Countering Violent Extremism in the Philippines

A Snapshot of Current Challenges and Responses

ASHLEY L. RHOADES, TODD C. HELMUS

NATIONAL SECURITY RESEARCH DIVISION

For more information on this publication, visit www.rand.org/t/RRA233-2

Library of Congress Cataloging-in-Publication Data is available for this publication.
ISBN: 978-1-9774-0572-2

Published by the RAND Corporation, Santa Monica, Calif.
© Copyright 2020 RAND Corporation
RAND® is a registered trademark.

Cover image: acrylic / Getty Images

Support RAND
Make a tax-deductible charitable contribution at
www.rand.org/giving/contribute

www.rand.org

Preface

In this report, we aim to provide policymakers and program implementers with helpful information on the threat landscape in the Philippines (in terms of active terrorist groups and drivers of radicalization) and raise awareness of Philippine government and nongovernmental programs in the countering violent extremism (CVE) space to inform the design and execution of such programming. This report is based on a review of open-source literature, not original research or fieldwork, and therefore should be read as an overview of existing challenges and responses rather than as an exhaustive examination of all CVE-related programming in the Philippines.

This research was sponsored by the Global Engagement Center at the U.S. Department of State and conducted within the International Security and Defense Policy Center of the RAND National Security Research Division (NSRD), which operates the National Defense Research Institute (NDRI), a federally funded research and development center sponsored by the Office of the Secretary of Defense, the Joint Staff, the Unified Combatant Commands, the Navy, the Marine Corps, the defense agencies, and the defense intelligence enterprise.

For more information on the RAND International Security and Defense Policy Center, see www.rand.org/nsrd/isdp or contact the director (contact information provided on the webpage).

Contents

Preface iii

Figures vii

Summary ix

Acknowledgments xi

Abbreviations xiii

CHAPTER ONE

Nature and Magnitude of the Threat 1

Nature of the Threat 2

Magnitude of the Threat 11

CHAPTER TWO

Drivers of Radicalization 19

Push Factors 19

Pull Factors 25

Push Versus Pull Factors 31

CHAPTER THREE

Countering Violent Extremism Programs and Initiatives 33

Types of CVE Programs and Initiatives 33

Lessons for CVE Efforts in the Philippines 45

Conclusion 50

References 51

Figures

1.1. Terrorist Attacks in the Philippines by Perpetrator,
      2001–2018 13
1.2. Casualties from Terrorist Attacks in the Philippines by
      Perpetrator, 2001–2018 14
1.3. Marawi After the 2017 Conflict 17

Summary

The threat of terrorism and violent extremism in the Philippines—especially in Mindanao, the country's second-largest island—is severe and persistent. In this report, we provide a snapshot of the terrorist and extremist threats facing the Philippines and the countering violent extremism (CVE) efforts that the Philippine government and nongovernmental agencies have undertaken in response.[1] We summarize the results of our review of these topics.

In Chapter One, we provide an overview of the various terrorist and extremist groups active within the Philippines and their histories, primary targets, operational methods, and geographic reach.

In Chapter Two, we document the push factors and pull factors that contribute to the radicalization process. Push factors include illiteracy, poverty, weak rule of law, inadequate social services, and limited economic opportunity. Pull factors, which play a particularly strong role in radicalization, include financial incentives, online propaganda,

---

[1] CVE focuses on preventing or diverting individuals from radicalizing to violence. Governments and implementing agencies use a variety of terms to refer to this concept, including *preventing violent extremism*, *countering radicalization*, and *terrorism prevention*. The U.S. Department of Homeland Security defines CVE as "proactive actions to counter efforts by extremists to recruit, radicalize, and mobilize followers to violence," noting that "fundamentally, CVE actions intend to address the conditions and reduce the factors that most likely contribute to recruitment and radicalization by violent extremists" (U.S. Department of Homeland Security, "Countering Violent Extremism Task Force—What Is CVE?" webpage, undated). The U.S. Department of State similarly describes CVE as being "a pillar of the Administration's strategic approach to counterterrorism, and . . . an increasingly critical component of a comprehensive and sustainable counterterrorism strategy that seeks to address the entire life cycle of radicalization to violent extremism" (U.S. Department of State, "Programs and Initiatives," webpage, undated).

and in-person recruitment networks. In addition, joining a militant group can provide power, camaraderie, and a sense of purpose. We cover the grievances that can prompt radicalization to violence, the vulnerable populations susceptible to radicalization, and terrorist and extremist organizations' recruitment tactics.

In Chapter Three, we document the main types of CVE efforts underway in the Philippines. The Philippine government focuses on military and counterterrorism operations; however, it also runs the Resilient Communities in Conflict-Affected Communities program. This program aims to improve local and national governance, reduce poverty, and improve the delivery of social services. In addition, the government runs counterradicalization programs in certain prison facilities. Regional and international cooperation efforts include the Association of Southeast Asian Nations Regional Forum Work Plan for Counter Terrorism and Transnational Crime. Community engagement programs aim to promote dialogue and cooperation between Muslim and Christian communities and educate the general public on CVE issues. Finally, local and international organizations conduct various countermessaging campaigns. We conclude this chapter by addressing the policy implications of these programs and highlighting some potential approaches and focuses for future CVE programming. We emphasize that CVE efforts should make a concerted effort to monitor and evaluate implementation so that other programming can benefit from lessons learned.

Acknowledgments

We are grateful to the numerous individuals and entities that supported the conduct of this research. In particular, we are grateful to the staff at Equal Access International, especially Exan Sharief and Ahmed Harris Pangcoga, who were our critical partners throughout the course of this research. We also thank Timothy Andrews and Jill Moss at the U.S. Department of State's Global Engagement Center for trusting the RAND Corporation with this work. Finally, we would like to thank Colin Clarke of Carnegie Mellon University and Jennifer Moroney of RAND for their helpful and insightful comments that improved the quality of this report. Any errors in this report are the sole responsibility of the authors.

Abbreviations

ABB	Alex Boncayao Brigade
AFP	Armed Forces of the Philippines
AFP-CMO	Armed Forces of the Philippines–Civil Military Operations Group
AKP	Ansar al-Khilafah
ARMM	Autonomous Region in Muslim Mindanao
ASEAN	Association of Southeast Asian Nations
ASG	Abu Sayyaf Group
ATC	Anti-Terrorism Council
BARMM	Bangsamoro Autonomous Region of Muslim Mindanao
BBL	Bangsamoro Basic Law
BIFF	Bangsamoro Islamic Freedom Fighters
CPP	Communist People's Party
CVE	countering violent extremism
EAI	Equal Access International
ISIS	Islamic State in Iraq and Syria
JIM	Justice for Islamic Movement
JSOTF-P	U.S. Joint Special Operations Task Force–Philippines
MILF	Moro Islamic Liberation Front
MNLF	Moro National Liberation Front

NDF   National Democratic Front
NGO   nongovernmental organization
NPA   New People's Army
PAMANA   *Payapa at Masaganang Pamayanan* (Resilient Communities in Conflict-Affected Communities)
PNP   Philippine National Police
RPA   Revolutionary Proletarian Army
RPM-P   *Rebolusyonaryong Partido ng Manggagawa ng Pilipinas*
SAF   Special Action Force
SOF   special operations forces
START   Study of Terrorism and Responses to Terrorism
USAID   U.S. Agency for International Development

CHAPTER ONE

Nature and Magnitude of the Threat

The Philippines' history of terrorism, insurgency, and other forms of ideologically motivated violence dates back to at least the 1970s, with the rise to prominence of the nation's first Muslim separatist and Communist militant groups. Although there is a great deal of literature covering various aspects of this history, we were unable to find a summary of the current dimensions of the terrorist threat and recent major attacks.

In this report, we provide a current threat picture (in terms of active terrorist groups and drivers of radicalization) to serve as a reference for those seeking to design programs or policies to counter violent extremism in the Philippines. We also want to raise awareness of recent and ongoing programs in the countering violent extremism (CVE) space to inform the design and execution of future programs.

We conducted a review of open-source literature for this report. Given this reliance on the literature, rather than original research or fieldwork, this report should be understood as an overview of existing challenges and responses, not as an exhaustive examination of all CVE-related programming in the Philippines.

In the following section, we describe the nature of the threats in the Philippines, providing information about the ideological sources of the threats and the array of terrorist and violent extremist groups actively operating throughout the Philippines. In the second section of this chapter, we address the magnitude of the threats, presenting data on major attacks, the geographic distribution of attacks, the distribution of attacks by perpetrator, the number of attacks, and the number of casualties.

Nature of the Threats

The roster and alignment of groups operating within the Philippines has fluctuated, but terrorists and rebels have been consistently motivated by two overarching ideologies: Islamist extremism and Communism. In this section, we provide an overview of all known groups of these ideologies that are actively operating at the time of writing. For each group, we provide information about its history, goals, estimated size, area of operation, and operational methods.

Islamist Terrorist and Violent Extremist Groups

During the last two decades, an eclectic mix of Islamist extremist groups has operated throughout the Philippines. These groups are unstable: They splinter frequently, occasionally converge in tactical alliances, and vacillate among committing criminal acts, mounting insurgency against the government, and carrying out terrorism as their primary pursuits. Although these groups vary in their specific motivations and strategies, the overarching political goal of these groups is to expel the Christian majority from Mindanao—the southernmost island group in the Philippines—and establish an autonomous or independent Islamic state there for Filipino Muslims, who are commonly referred to as the *Moro* or *Bangsamoro* people.[1] Although some groups have managed to execute attacks in the capital city of Manila and, venturing beyond Philippine borders, in Malaysia and the surrounding seas, most Islamist terrorist activity in the Philippines is confined to Mindanao and the neighboring Sulu Archipelago.[2]

The **Moro National Liberation Front (MNLF)** is the oldest Islamic extremist group in the Philippines. It was established in 1971 to fight for an independent Muslim Mindanao.[3] For many years, the

---

[1]   Stanford University, Center for International Security and Cooperation, "Moro National Liberation Front," webpage, last updated August 2019b.

[2]   Stanford University, Center for International Security and Cooperation, "Abu Sayyaf Group," webpage, last updated August 2018a.

[3]   Christopher Paul, Colin P. Clarke, Beth Grill, and Molly Dunigan, *Paths to Victory: Lessons from Modern Insurgencies*, Santa Monica, Calif.: RAND Corporation, RR-291/1-OSD, 2013, p. 43.

MNLF led the armed Muslim separatist campaign against the government. At its peak in 1975, the MNLF had about 30,000 members; membership had dropped to about 17,700 by 1996.[4] The MNLF signed a peace agreement with the Philippine government in 1996.[5] Since then, the MNLF has sporadically engaged in political activities and violent attacks, but its popularity has declined, and it has largely been sidelined in further negotiations with the government.[6] As the goalposts in the struggle for Moro independence have shifted, several groups have split from the MNLF and have in turn produced their own splinter groups.

The **Moro Islamic Liberation Front (MILF)**—which split from the MNLF in 1978 to pursue a more Islam-focused agenda in conjunction with the quest for Moro independence—supplanted the MNLF as the primary organization conducting negotiations with the Philippine government for a Muslim autonomous region.[7] Although the group entered into a ceasefire agreement with the government in 1997, the ceasefire has collapsed several times since, with the MILF conducting terrorist attacks as recently as 2017.[8] Size estimates for the MILF have varied greatly. The most recent estimate is about 10,000 militants, although the group has reportedly been disarming and decommissioning some members in accordance with agreements negotiated with the government.[9]

As the MILF began to adopt a more favorable stance toward autonomy, as opposed to complete independence, more-radical factions

---

[4] Stanford University, Center for International Security and Cooperation, 2019b.

[5] Rommel C. Banlaoi, "Current Terrorist Groups and Emerging Extremist Armed Movements in the Southern Philippines," in Fermin R. De Leon, Jr., and Ernesto R. Aradanas, *National Security Review, The Study of National Security at 50: Reawakenings*, Quezon City: National Defense College of the Philippines, 2013, p. 174.

[6] Stanford University, Center for International Security and Cooperation, 2019b.

[7] Stanford University, Center for International Security and Cooperation, "Moro Islamic Liberation Front," webpage, last updated August 2019a.

[8] Stanford University, Center for International Security and Cooperation, 2019a.

[9] Stanford University, Center for International Security and Cooperation, 2019a; Gerg Cahiles, "Expert Doubts MILF Combatants Will Disarm Completely," *CNN Philippines*, June 17, 2015.

split from the group. One such faction is the **Bangsamoro Islamic Freedom Fighters (BIFF)**, which split from the MILF in 2010 and declared its allegiance to the **Islamic State of Iraq and Syria (ISIS)** in July 2014.[10] The BIFF has been more brutal in its tactics and selection of targets, attacking civilians and government forces in an effort to undermine negotiations between the MILF and the Philippine government.[11] In 2013, the BIFF's leader, Mohammad Ali Tambako, left to form a new group, the **Justice for Islamic Movement (JIM)**, purportedly in reaction to disagreements within the BIFF over his decision to attack civilian communities.[12] The BIFF and JIM have since reconciled and formed an alliance against the Philippine government.[13]

The MILF produced another splinter group at about the same time that the BIFF emerged. This second new group was known as the **Maute Group** or the **Islamic State in Lanao**. The Maute Group was founded by two brothers from the province of Lanao del Sur in Mindanao, Omar and Abdullah Maute, who reportedly had familial ties to MILF leadership as well as strong ties to ISIS, to which the group pledged allegiance in 2015.[14] Some sources indicate that the Maute Group's ranks included foreign fighters from Indonesia and Malaysia and that the group might have received funding from Indonesian and Syrian sources.[15] Although the group only had an estimated 300 fighters at its peak, it was surprisingly successful in battling the Philippine military, and it garnered attention as a particularly dangerous fac-

---

[10] Stanford University, Center for International Security and Cooperation, "Bangsamoro Islamic Freedom Fighters," webpage, last updated August 2018b.

[11] Stanford University, Center for International Security and Cooperation, 2018b.

[12] Stanford University, Center for International Security and Cooperation, "Mapping Militants—Philippines," data set, undated.

[13] Stanford University, Center for International Security and Cooperation, undated.

[14] Jonathan Head, "Maute Rebel Group: A Rising Threat to Philippines," *BBC News*, May 31, 2017.

[15] Head, 2017; Patrick B. Johnston and Colin P. Clarke, "Is the Philippines the Next Caliphate?" *Foreign Policy*, November 27, 2017; International Crisis Group, *The Philippines: Militancy and the New Bangsamoro*, Brussels, Asia Report No. 301, July 27, 2019.

tion.[16] In October 2017, the Maute brothers, along with several other members of the group, were killed while fighting against government forces in the city of Marawi.[17] After this fight, Abu Dar, one of the planners of the battle, briefly assumed leadership of the group before being killed in April 2019 as part of the military crackdown on terrorist groups championed by President Rodrigo Duterte.[18] Since then, the Maute Group has largely disbanded, with the remaining members reportedly joining ISIS-Philippines.[19]

Perhaps the most notorious extremist group in the Philippines is the **Abu Sayyaf Group (ASG)**, which parted ways with the MNLF in 1991 to form the smallest but most radical of the MNLF's splinter groups.[20] The ASG was the first Filipino Islamist extremist organization to be named to the U.S. Department of State's list of foreign terrorist organizations, having been designated in 1997.[21] The ASG initially drew ideological inspiration, funding, and training from al Qaeda. Its founder, Abdurajak Abubakar Janjalani, had a personal connection to Osama bin Laden; bin Laden's brother-in-law provided funding to the ASG early on, and the architect of the 9/11 attacks, Khalid Shaikh Mohammed, helped train members of the ASG.[22] However, the ASG joined the BIFF in pledging allegiance to ISIS through videos posted

---

[16] Head, 2017; Michael Hart, "A Year After Marawi, What's Left of ISIS in the Philippines?" *The Diplomat*, October 25, 2018.

[17] Julmunir I. Jannaral, "7 Maute Brothers Confirmed Dead," *Manila Times*, December 6, 2017; Hart, 2018.

[18] Catherine S. Valente, "Duterte to Military: Crush NPA, Other Enemies," *Manila Times*, December 18, 2019; Carmela Fonbuena, "Leader of Isis in Philippines Killed, DNA Tests Confirm," *The Guardian*, April 14, 2019.

[19] "Outcome Document: The Role of Parliamentarians in Preventing and Countering Terrorism and Addressing Conditions Conducive to Terrorism in the Asia-Pacific Region," Inter-Parliamentary Union–United Nations Regional Conference, Kuala Lumpur, October 1–3, 2019.

[20] McKenzie O'Brien, "Fluctuations Between Crime and Terror: The Case of Abu Sayyaf's Kidnapping Activities," *Terrorism and Political Violence*, Vol. 24, No. 2, 2012, p. 321.

[21] U.S. Department of State, Bureau of Counterterrorism, "Foreign Terrorist Organizations," webpage, undated.

[22] Stanford University, 2018a.

on social media in July 2014, straining its relationship with al Qaeda.[23] ISIS has since taken credit for several ASG attacks, as well as attacks by other rebel groups in the Philippines. Despite its origin as part of the MNLF and its connections to al Qaeda and ISIS, for much of its existence, the ASG has engaged primarily in violent criminal behavior with no clear political or ideological agenda other than material gain.[24] Because of its violent activities and extremist ideology, the ASG has never been included in peace negotiations with the government. The ASG finances itself through kidnapping, blackmail, extortion, smuggling, and marijuana sales; it has provided some funds to local communities to cultivate support.[25] ASG leader Isnilon Hapilon was killed by the Armed Forces of the Philippines (AFP) in October 2017, rendering the future of the group uncertain.[26] By 2018, the Philippine government estimated that the organization's membership had fallen to fewer than 150 members, a significant decline from its peak membership of about 1,250 in 2000.[27] After waging a fierce campaign against the group, the Philippine government claimed in early 2019 that the ASG had only 20 members left.[28]

Beyond the MNLF umbrella, other Islamist extremist groups targeting the Philippines include **Ansar al-Khilafah (AKP)**, which emerged in 2014 through a video pledging allegiance to ISIS, and the Indonesian, al Qaeda–affiliated terrorist network **Jemaah Islamiyah**,

[23] Stanford University, Center for International Security and Cooperation, 2018a.

[24] Stanford University, Center for International Security and Cooperation, 2018a; Banlaoi, undated, p. 165.

[25] The Mackenzie Institute, "Terrorism Profiles: Abu Sayyaf Group," webpage, last updated November 13, 2015.

[26] Felipe Villamor, "Philippines Says It Killed ISIS-Linked Leader in Push to Reclaim City," *New York Times,* October 16, 2017.

[27] Stanford University, Center for International Security and Cooperation, 2018a; Francis Wakefield, "Government Troops Still Chasing 150 Abu Sayyaf Terrorists—Lorenzana," *Manila Bulletin*, August 28, 2018.

[28] Hannah Beech and Jason Gutierrez, "How ISIS Is Rising in the Philippines as It Dwindles in the Middle East," *New York Times*, March 12, 2019.

which occasionally collaborates with select Filipino terrorist groups or works alone to conduct attacks against Philippine targets.[29]

In addition to influencing and supporting other jihadist groups in the region, ISIS has established its own branch in the Philippines (**ISIS-Philippines**), earning its own designation on the U.S. Department of State's foreign terrorist organizations list in February 2018.[30] ISIS-Philippines is undeniably an important element of the jihadist landscape in the Philippines because of the messaging strategies, funding streams, and branding associated with the ISIS name.[31] In 2016, ISIS began calling for recruits to join the jihad in the Philippines instead of its Iraq- and Syria-based caliphate, prompting fighters from across the globe to take up arms and travel to the Philippines.[32] That same year, now-deceased ISIS leader Abu Bakr al-Baghdadi dubbed Hapilon as an emir of ISIS in East Asia. Baghdadi also designated several smaller Philippine-based groups, which had pledged loyalty to ISIS, as official ISIS brigades.[33] Since 2016, the burgeoning ISIS-Philippines has subsumed militants from several other groups in the Philippines, blurring the lines between some of the organizations and complicating attribution of attacks. ISIS-Philippines was instrumental in orchestrating the siege of Marawi in 2017, and ISIS-affiliated militants managed to capture the city at the outset of the battle.[34] Despite its eventual defeat in Marawi at the hands of the Philippine military, ISIS spun its initial victory to its advantage, featuring the battle heavily in its recruitment propaganda.[35] We have no credible estimates of the group's size, partly because of its nebulous relationships with other groups in the region.

---

[29] Caleb Weiss, "Philippines-Based Jihadist Groups Pledge Allegiance to the Islamic State," *FDD's Long War Journal*, February 14, 2016.

[30] U.S. Department of State, Bureau of Counterterrorism, undated.

[31] Zachary Abuza and Colin P. Clarke, "The Islamic State Meets Southeast Asia," *Foreign Affairs*, September 16, 2019.

[32] Beech and Gutierrez, 2019.

[33] Abuza and Clarke, 2019.

[34] Devin Lurie, "ISIS in the Philippines: A Cause for Concern," *American Security Project*, June 4, 2020.

[35] Lurie, 2020.

However, it appears that ISIS has been very successful in its recruitment efforts, preying on vulnerable individuals throughout the Philippines and capitalizing on deep grievances with the government.[36] The group's terror tactics emulate those of ISIS's Middle East branch. It relies heavily on suicide bombings against Philippine government and civilian targets (particularly Catholic establishments) and U.S.-affiliated targets (namely the U.S. embassy).[37] According to one analysis, the Philippines' landscape of Islamic extremist actors, combined with its vulnerable populations alienated from the government, have made the country "ISIS' greatest hope for a revival of its caliphate."[38]

As the history of Islamist terrorist groups in the Philippines illustrates, it is common for splinter groups, factions within larger groups, and reconstituted groups to emerge. It is entirely plausible that the remaining adherents of weakened groups, such as the Maute Group, could reconstitute to form a successor group, even while they continue to pledge allegiance to ISIS.

Communist Terrorist and Violent Extremist Groups

Although the Philippine government's efforts to counter and contain the Islamist extremist separatist movement have taken center stage in recent years, the government's longest-running campaign has been against the Communist coalition formed by the **Communist People's Party (CPP)**; its armed wing, called the **New People's Army (NPA)**; and its political wing, called the **National Democratic Front (NDF)**.[39] The Maoist-inspired CPP was founded in 1968 by student activists in Manila and seeks to refute the influence of U.S. imperialism, capitalism, and feudalism through a revolution by the masses.[40] The NPA was founded a year later in 1969 to help accomplish this

---

[36] Abuza and Clarke, 2019.

[37] Lurie, 2020.

[38] Abuza and Clarke, 2019.

[39] Banlaoi, undated, p. 170.

[40] "The New People's Army," *Terrorism*, Vol. 13, No. 2, 1990.

goal by starting an armed revolution to overthrow the government.[41] In 1973, the CPP-NPA established the NDF as an umbrella organization to unify several existing Communist and revolutionary organizations.[42] In addition, because the CPP-NPA has rejected legal political activity in favor of armed struggle, it uses the NDF as an intermediary to negotiate with the government. Meanwhile, the political party and its armed wing have become largely synonymous, and the U.S. Department of State designated the CPP-NPA as a single foreign terrorist organization in 2002.[43] The CPP-NPA has members throughout the Philippines, including in Manila, and, as of 2009, it had just shy of 5,000 members, down from its strength of 25,200 in its 1987 heyday.[44] The CPP-NPA has launched more terrorist attacks than any other group in the Philippines, and it has a wider geographic reach within the Philippines than its Islamist extremist counterparts.[45] The CPP-NPA has also conducted attacks in Mindanao, but its strongest presence is on the islands of Luzon—particularly in the regions of Calabarzon and Mimaropa—and the Visayas.[46]

The 1980s saw the emergence of two CPP-NPA splinter groups: the **Alex Boncayao Brigade (ABB)** and the **Revolutionary Proletarian Army (RPA)**.[47] The ABB had been a faction within the CPP-NPA, serving as the group's guerrilla force in Manila, but it decided to leave the group because of ideological and tactical differences. During the 1980s and 1990s, the ABB assassinated more than 100 people in the Philippines—likely including a U.S. Army colonel. More recently, it claimed credit for 2,000 attacks on the Department of Energy in

---

[41] Stanford University, Center for International Security and Cooperation, "Communist Party of the Philippines—New People's Army," webpage, last updated August 2018c.

[42] Banlaoi, undated, p. 170.

[43] Counter Extremism Project, *The Philippines: Extremism and Counter-Extremism*, New York, undated b, p. 1; U.S. Department of State, Bureau of Counterterrorism, undated.

[44] Counter Extremism Project, undated b, p. 1.

[45] Study of Terrorism and Responses to Terrorism (START) Global Terrorism Database, data set, undated.

[46] Stanford University, Center for International Security and Cooperation, 2018c.

[47] Stanford University, Center for International Security and Cooperation, undated.

Manila and the Shell Oil offices in the central Philippines.[48] The RPA purportedly left the CPP-NPA for similar reasons, although less is known about the group. In 1997, the ABB and RPA converged to form a political arm called the ***Rebolusyonaryong Partido ng Manggagawà ng Pilipinas*** (**RPM-P**).[49] The RPM-P entered into a peace agreement with the Philippine government in 2000, and it has even engaged in legitimate politics by entering candidates in elections.[50] The ABB and RPA continue to act as the RPM-P's armed wing, but they have not perpetrated any major attacks in recent years.

Other Sources of Threat

In addition to the conflicts propagated by these militant groups, local-level rivalries (known as *rido*) between different families, political parties, and ethnic groups can contribute to outbreaks of violence within communities.[51]

The Philippine government also has flagged foreign fighters as an area of concern. Filipino citizens could become radicalized to fight abroad and potentially return to the Philippines, and non-Filipino foreign fighters could become engaged in the Philippines, as happened in Marawi.[52] The exact numbers of outgoing and returning foreign fighters are not available, but it has been widely reported that hundreds of people from Southeast Asia, including at least some members of the ASG and other Islamist extremist groups, were deployed to Syria to fight against the Assad regime; some of these fighters eventu-

---

[48] FAS Intelligence Resource Program, "Alex Boncayo Brigade (ABB)," webpage, May 21, 2004; Colleen Sullivan, "Alex Boncayo Brigade," *Encyclopedia Britannica*, undated.

[49] Stanford University, Center for International Security and Cooperation, undated.

[50] Stanford University, Center for International Security and Cooperation, undated.

[51] Asia Foundation, *Transforming Conflicts in Sulu and Basilan Through People-to-People Engagement*, Makati City, Philippines, 2013, p. 3; Elieso F. Huesca, Jr., "On 'Youth, Peace, and Security' in Mindanao, Philippines," *Peace Review*, Vol. 31, 2019, p. 59.

[52] Several scholars have echoed these concerns about returning foreign fighters. See Daveed Gartenstein-Ross and Colin P. Clarke, "What Do Returning Isis Fighters Do Next? You're About to Find Out," *This Week in Asia*, February 2, 2020.

ally returned to their countries of origin.[53] The Philippine government reportedly identified more than 30 combatants killed in Marawi as foreign fighters, and some terrorism experts estimate that an additional 100 foreign fighters from 16 countries have entered Mindanao since the battle ended.[54] Filipinos have also been featured in ISIS videos, with one Filipino ISIS member supposedly participating in the beheading of 18 Syrian Air Force pilots and U.S. citizen Peter Kassig in November 2014.[55] This same individual also allegedly appeared in a video encouraging Filipino jihadists to come to Iraq and Syria to fight for ISIS.[56]

Magnitude of the Threat

The Philippines faces a very high level of threat from terrorist and extremist activity, ranking in ninth place on the Global Terrorism Index's 2019 list of countries most affected by terrorism.[57] In this section, we provide data on attacks, casualties, and geographic distribution of attacks and a breakdown of attacks by perpetrator post-9/11. We also provide an overview of major attacks during this period.

Trends in Terrorist Attacks

Since 9/11, the Philippines has experienced 4,039 terrorist plots by Islamist and Communist extremist groups; 3,350 of these plots were

---

[53] Daveed Gartenstein-Ross, Colin P. Clarke, and Samuel Hodgson, *Foreign Terrorist Fighters from Southeast Asia: What Happens Next?* The Hague: International Center for Counter-Terrorism, February 17, 2020.

[54] Zam Yusa, "Philippines: 100 Foreign Fighters Joined ISIS in Mindanao Since the Marawi Battle," *Defense Post*, November 5, 2018; Hannah Ellis-Petersen and Carmela Fonbuena, "Philippines: Scores of Islamic State Fighters on Mindanao Island," *The Guardian*, November 11, 2018.

[55] Counter Extremism Project, undated b, p. 3; Judith Tinnes, "Although the (Dis-)Believers Dislike It: A Backgrounder on IS Hostage Videos—August–December 2014," *Perspectives on Terrorism*, Vol. 9, No. 1, February 2015.

[56] Counter Extremism Project, undated b, p. 3.

[57] Institute for Economics and Peace, *Global Terrorism Index 2019: Measuring the Index of Terrorism*, Sydney, November 2019, p. 8.

successfully executed.[58] Islamist and Communist groups have at times collaborated on attacks, especially when fighting against the Philippine Army in Mindanao. The loss of life from these attacks has been staggering; During 2001–2018, at least 7,671 Filipinos were killed or injured by terrorist attacks (stemming from all ideological sources). The CPP-NPA's decades of armed "revolution" against the government have to date resulted in the loss of more than 120,000 lives.[59] The CPA-NPA has committed the most attacks since 9/11, launching 1,161 attacks and killing or injuring 993 people.[60] However, Islamist extremist groups inflicted the highest number of casualties from 2011 to 2018, with 2,264 deaths and injuries (MILF attacks killed and injured 1,173, BIFF attacks 586, and ASG attacks 505).[61] Figures 1.1 and 1.2 depict the number of terrorist attacks by all groups that took place each year, as well as the associated death toll from September 12, 2001, through December 31, 2018 (the last day for which data are available).

Major Attacks

This section provides an overview of the major attacks that have occurred in the Philippines from 9/11 to the present. In a bid to strengthen its negotiating position with the government, the MILF has conducted several major attacks, including bombing civilian and government targets and taking hostages. Its most fatal attacks include setting off a bomb at the Davao City International Airport in 2003, killing 22 and wounding 148; attacking and decapitating several Philippine Marines who were trying to rescue a hostage held by the ASG in 2007, killing 18 to 43 people and wounding at least nine more; and attacking Philippine National Police (PNP) Special Action Force (SAF) troopers in 2015, killing about 67 and wounding 12 others.[62]

---

[58] START Global Terrorism Database, undated.

[59] START Global Terrorism Database, undated; Frank Cibulka, "The Philippines: In the Eye of the Political Storm," in Daljit Singh and Lorraine C. Salazar, eds., *Southeast Asian Affairs 2007*, Singapore: Institute of Southeast Asian Affairs, 2007, p. 267.

[60] START Global Terrorism Database, undated.

[61] START Global Terrorism Database, undated.

[62] Stanford University, Center for International Security and Cooperation, 2019a.

Figure 1.1
Terrorist Attacks in the Philippines by Perpetrator, 2001–2018

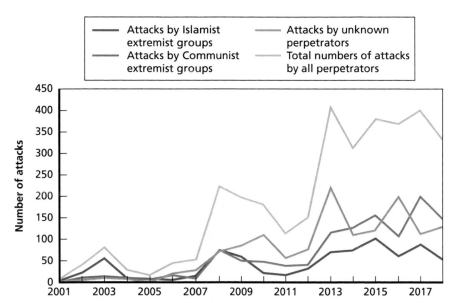

SOURCE: Data were derived from the START Global Terrorism Database, undated.
NOTES: We coded attacks solely based on the group that START Global Terrorism Database designated as the primary perpetrator of the attack. In a handful of instances, there were multiple perpetrators behind an attack, with Islamist extremist groups and Communist extremist groups colluding. These attacks were not double counted across categories. We coded them only as an attack by an Islamist extremist group, by a communist or left-wing extremist group, or by an unknown perpetrator.

In January 2017, 100 MILF- and BIFF-linked militants stormed the North Cotabato District Jail on Mindanao, engaging in a shoot-out with guards and enabling the escape of more than 150 inmates.[63]

The ASG has conducted numerous bombings, assassinations, kidnappings for ransom, beheadings, monetary extortions of businesses and individuals, murders, and robberies. The ASG's primary targets are Christians, foreigners (particularly Westerners), and the Philippine military.[64] The ASG has perpetrated several high-fatality bomb-

---

[63] Counter Extremism Project, undated b, p. 5.

[64] Counter Extremism Project, "Abu Sayyaf Group (ASG)," webpage, undated a.

Figure 1.2
Casualties from Terrorist Attacks in the Philippines by Perpetrator, 2001–2018

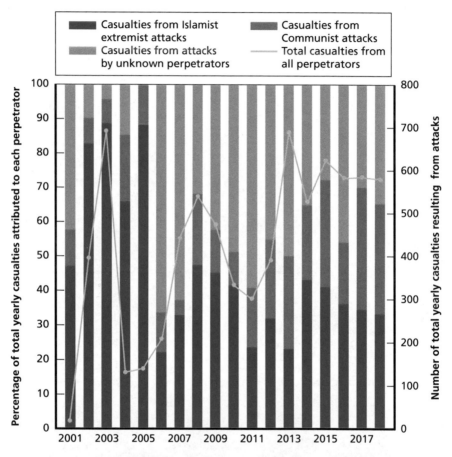

SOURCE: Data were derived from the START Global Terrorism Database, undated.
NOTE: The casualty count includes both fatalities and nonlethal injuries.

ings against both government and civilian targets, including the 2002 Zamboanga City bombing; the 2005 Valentine's Day bombings in several Philippine cities; and the 2004 Super Ferry bombing in Manila Bay, which killed 116 people, making it the deadliest terrorist attack at sea.[65] The ASG was also behind a slew of kidnappings in 2016, and it has demonstrated its willingness to follow through on threats to behead individuals when the demanded ransom is not received, as illustrated by the beheadings of Canadian hostages John Ridsdel and Robert Hall in 2016.[66] The ASG seemingly collaborated with AKP and the Maute Group to execute the Davao market bombing in September 2016, which killed 15 people and injured about 70 more.[67] The ASG also collaborated with the MILF in the 2003 Davao City International Airport bombing.[68]

The Maute Group also committed several terrorist attacks in Mindanao in 2016, including the attempted bombing of the U.S. embassy in November 2016 and the December 2016 bombings in Leyte (an island in the central Philippines), which injured 23 civilians. [69]

During the last few years, ISIS-Philippines has conducted or claimed credit for several attacks, most notably the Marawi siege; a July 2018 suicide bombing at a checkpoint in the province of Basilan, which killed ten people; and the January 2019 suicide bombing of a Catholic cathedral, which killed 23 people.[70] The rise of ISIS-Philippines has made suicide bombing (long a preferred tactic of ISIS) a more-common form of attack in the Philippines.[71]

---

[65] Stanford University, Center for International Security and Cooperation, 2019a.

[66] Sarah W. Craun, Mark J. Rossin, and Matthew R. Collier, "Interpretations of Proof-of-Life Videos and Their Impact on Supported Interventions," *Journal of Policing, Intelligence and Counter Terrorism*, Vol. 14, No. 2, 2019.

[67] Counter Extremism Project, undated b, p. 5; "Philippines: Bomb Attack on Davao Market Kills 14," *BBC News*, September 3, 2016.

[68] Christoph Schuck, "How Islamist Is the Abu Sayyaf Group (ASG)? An Ideological Assessment," *Asian Security*, 2020.

[69] Caleb Weiss, "Filipino Troops Battle Islamic State–Loyal Forces for Town," *Threat Matrix: A Blog of FDD's Long War Journal*, November 29, 2016b.

[70] Beech and Gutierrez, 2019; U.S. Department of State, *Country Reports on Terrorism 2018*, Washington, D.C., 2018.

[71] Quinton Temby, "Cells, Factions and Suicide Operatives: The Fragmentation of Militant Islamism in the Philippines Post-Marawi," *Contemporary Southeast Asia: A Journal of International and Strategic Affairs*, Vol. 41, No. 1, 2019.

The CPP-NPA has perpetrated numerous bombings, assassinations, kidnappings, extortions, and other forms of violent attack against civilian and government targets. For example, in August 2011, a band of CPP-NPA militants kidnapped the mayor of the town of Lingig in the province of Surigao del Sur. They then forced him to apologize for what the group claimed were human rights abuses before releasing him.[72] In October 2011, the CPP-NPA attacked three mining sites in the province of Surigao del Norte to punish the companies that ran the sites for failing to pay their "revolutionary taxes to the CPP-NPA."[73] The attack caused an estimated $68 million worth of damage to the mining infrastructure, and a number of people were killed in the course of the attack.[74] In 2013, CPP-NPA militants attacked a vehicle carrying policemen and civilians, killing nine people and wounding 12 more.[75] Most recently, in February 2020, CPA-NPA militants fired a grenade launcher on a community in Surigao del Sur, wounding three civilians.[76]

The largest-scale attacks by Islamist extremist rebels in recent history occurred during the Marawi siege. In May 2017, Maute Group rebels, joined by fighters from ISIS-Philippines, AKP, the ASG, and other Islamist extremist groups, clashed with the AFP and the PNP, which had entered Marawi in search of Hapilon.[77] ASG's participation in the battle has led some to speculate that it may be shifting from primarily criminal activities to insurgent activities.[78] In the course of the battle, the Maute Group abducted civilians and used them as human shields, occupied the city hall and a hospital, and destroyed a Catholic

---

[72] Stanford University, Center for International Security and Cooperation, 2018c.

[73] Stanford University, Center for International Security and Cooperation, 2018c.

[74] Banlaoi, undated, pp. 170–171.

[75] Stanford University, Center for International Security and Cooperation, 2018c.

[76] Alexander Lopez, "Army, IP Leaders Hit NPA Attack on Civilians in Surigao Sur," Philippines News Agency, February 24, 2020.

[77] Joseph Franco, *Marawi: Winning the War After the Battle*, The Hague: International Centre for Counter-Terrorism, November 29, 2017.

[78] Banlaoi, undated, p. 165.

cathedral. By the end of the battle, 900 militants had been killed and about 400,000 residents had been displaced.[79] Figure 1.3 illustrates the devastating level of damage the city of Marawi sustained during this conflict.

Figure 1.3
Marawi After the 2017 Conflict

SOURCES: Photos courtesy of Zia Alonto Adiong (left) and Tirmizy Abdullah (right).

---

[79] International Institute for Strategic Studies, *Asia-Pacific Regional Security Assessment 2018*, Washington, D.C., June 2018.

CHAPTER TWO

Drivers of Radicalization

Drivers of radicalization in the Philippines consist primarily of *push factors* that steer an individual down the path of violent extremism—such as socioeconomic pressures—and *pull factors* that attract an individual to the idea of joining a terrorist or violent extremist group—such as propaganda and recruitment efforts.

Push Factors

There is no consensus on which push factor is the most important in radicalization. However, most CVE scholars and practitioners agree that the main drivers of radicalization in the Philippines—as in many other countries with radicalization issues—are poverty and economic hardship, ethnic and religious marginalization and disenfranchisement, and frustration with the government.[1]

Poverty and Economic Hardship
Poverty plagues many parts of the Philippines, and Muslims live in some of the most impoverished provinces. Some Muslims claimed they have been pushed toward Islamist extremist groups because they felt that the state was not providing for them and, in some cases, was

---

[1] Thomas Koruth Samuel, *Radicalisation in Southeast Asia: A Selected Case Study of Daesh in Indonesia, Malaysia, and the Philippines*, Kuala Lumpur: Southeast Asia Regional Centre for Counter-Terrorism, 2016, p. 96.

actively discriminating against them in matters of jobs and housing.[2] Some scholars have assessed that the primary drivers of violence and radicalization among Muslims in the Philippines are

> economic marginalization and destitution, political domina-
> tion, physical insecurity, threatened Moro and Islamic identity,
> a perception that government is the culprit[,] and a perception of
> hopelessness under the present order of things.[3]

Lack of education, which often goes hand in hand with poverty, also contributes to radicalization.[4] According to one analysis,

> there are only two ways for young males to command community
> respect in Mindanao's militarized zones: to take up arms or to get
> a good education. With intermittent violence hindering children
> from access to education, becoming "soldiers of Islam" or secu-
> rity bodyguards of political warlords are considered the shortest
> routes to gain "authority" in their own villages.[5]

Rural or suburban youth may be particularly susceptible to radicalization, as they tend to be both impoverished and uneducated. Many rural youth reportedly do not stay in school and work as day laborers on farms instead, leading to a large population of out-of-school youth who might view extremist organizations as their only prospect for success.[6] According to a 2017 survey, the largest grievances in the southern Philippines were lack of livelihoods and lack of food.[7] Another study found that violence in Mindanao tended to peak during agriculturally

---

[2]   Samuel, 2016, p. 97.

[3]   Raymundo B. Ferrer and Randolph G. Cabangnag, "Non-International Armed Conflicts in the Philippines," *International Law Studies*, Vol. 88, No. 1, 2012, p 267.

[4]   Samuel, 2016, p. 97.

[5]   Huesca, 2019, pp. 61–62.

[6]   Impl. Project, "Radicalization Trends and Findings in Mindanao," briefing, 2017b, slide 14.

[7]   Impl. Project, "2017 Annual Data Review: Marawi and Suburbs, Southern Philippines," briefing, 2017a, slide 18.

lean months and local elections, suggesting that conflict over resources and political issues are key drivers of radicalization to violence.[8] Conversely, a study of insurgency and unemployment that included the Philippines found that greater levels of unemployment were associated with less political violence (although they did contribute to higher levels of violence overall).[9]

The overall conditions in Mindanao—which is rife with conflict and has the highest levels of illiteracy and poverty as well as "weak rule of law and poor accountability, inadequate social services, and limited economic opportunity"—have created an environment in which radical thought and further violence can thrive.[10] The World Bank found that the five provinces of the Bangsamoro Autonomous Region of Muslim Mindanao (BARMM) are among the most impoverished in the Philippines, with an incidence of poverty up to 25 percent higher than in the rest of the Philippines.[11] Another study found that the BARMM provinces scored significantly below the national average in the Human Development Index, which measures per capita income, life expectancy, and education levels.[12] The ongoing conflict in Mindanao has worsened existing issues and provided the ideal context for radicalization to take root.

---

[8] Ever J. Abasolo, *Applying a Violence Intensity Index in the Bangsamoro*, London: International Alert, 2014, p. 6.

[9] Eli Berman, Michael Callan, Joseph H. Felter, and Jacob N. Shapiro, "Do Working Men Rebel? Insurgency and Unemployment in Afghanistan, Iraq, and the Philippines," *Journal of Conflict Resolution*, Vol. 55, No. 4, 2011, pp. 496–528.

[10] U.S. Agency for International Development (USAID), "Our Work in Mindanao," webpage, July 6, 2018; Leah Angela V. Robis, "The Sun Rises Anew in Mindanao: Towards Recognizing the Bangsamoro Nation Within the Context of the Philippine Republic," *Ateneo Law Journal*, Vol. 59, No. 4, 2015.

[11] World Bank, "Philippines: Autonomous Region in Muslim Mindanao (ARMM Social Fund Project)," webpage, April 10, 2013.

[12] Joseph J. Capuno, "Probing Conflict Contagion and Casualties in Mindanao, Philippines," *Defense and Peace Economics*, 2019, p. 4.

Ethnic and Religious Marginalization

Another driver of radicalization is the deep cultural and geographical divide between Christian and Muslim communities in the Philippines, which has been exacerbated by anti-Muslim stereotypes and resentment over military operations perceived to prejudicially target Muslims. The Philippines is a predominantly Catholic society. Islam is the second-largest religion in the Philippines, but only about 6 percent of the population is Muslim.[13] The vast majority of the Philippines's Muslim population—comprising 13 ethnic groups—lives on the island of Mindanao, geographically isolated from Christian communities.[14] In addition, more than 20 indigenous groups that are not Muslim (known as *Lumads*) live in Mindanao. They are largely socially isolated from—and sometimes ostracized by—both Muslim and Christian populations.[15]

Although the Philippine government nominally affords Muslims a substantial degree of religious freedom and tolerance, some Filipino Muslims have expressed that they view Christians resettling in traditionally Muslim areas, such as Mindanao, as an encroachment on their religious and cultural identity.[16] Some members of the Muslim community are wary of the Philippine military, viewing it as an enforcement arm of the largely Christian government that frequently profiles all Muslims as terrorists.[17] According to a researcher who interviewed youth who had joined the MILF, many interviewees indicated that

---

[13] U.S. Department of State, 2018; Philippine Statistics Authority, Region XI—Davao Region, "Factsheet on Islam in Mindanao," webpage, September 28, 2017.

[14] U.S. Department of State, 2018; Matteo Vergani, "Neojihadism and Muslim–Christian Relations in the Mindanao Resistance Movement: A Study of Facebook Digital Narratives," *Islam and Christian–Muslim Relations*, Vol. 25, No. 3, 2014, p. 359.

[15] Vergani, 2014.

[16] U.S. Department of State, Bureau of Democracy, Human Rights and Labor, *Philippine 2013 International Religious Freedom Report*, Washington, D.C., 2013.

[17] Diana Dunham-Scott, *Understanding and Engaging the Muslims of the Southern Philippines*, dissertation, Pardee RAND Graduate School, Santa Monica, Calif.: RAND Corporation, RGSD-301, 2012.

their adherence to ethnoreligious ideology was a major factor in their decision to join the group.[18]

Meanwhile, the Christian majority has long perceived Muslims as being "troublemakers and violent," and many closely, if falsely, associate Muslims with terrorism, particularly because of the high level of terrorist activity in Muslim areas of Mindanao.[19] Indeed, attacks by Islamist extremist groups have exacerbated tensions between the Muslim and Christian communities, with both sides feeling persecuted either by the attacks themselves or by the government's often heavy-handed militant response, which has grown even harsher under the leadership of Duterte.[20]

Frustration with the Government

For decades, various extremist groups have been in on-and-off negotiations with the government over the status of Mindanao. The lack of an arrangement for an independent, Muslim Mindanao that satisfies all parties to the conflict has been a major grievance and driver of radicalization. In 1989, after years of fighting and negotiating with the MNLF and the MILF, the Philippine government passed Republic Act No. 6734, establishing the Autonomous Region in Muslim Mindanao (ARMM).[21] The ARMM included five provinces—Basilan, Lanao del Sur, Maguindanao, Sulu, and Tawi-Tawi—and two cities, Marawi

---

[18] Huesca, 2019, p. 60.

[19] Raul Dancel, "Marawi a Crucible of Filipino Identity," *Straits Times,* January 18, 2018; Manuel Mogato and Karen Lema, "Philippine Muslims Fear Marawi Fighting May Deepen Communal Discord," Reuters, June 28, 2017; Harry Cockburn, "Philippines: Muslims 'Being Profiled' Under Martial Law," *The Independent,* August 20, 2017.

[20] Zachary Abuza, "Duterte Thinks He Can Bomb Islamists into Submission. He Cannot," *New York Times,* June 21, 2017; Jesse Chase-Lubitz, "Duterte's War on Terror Also Looks Like a War on Civilians," *Foreign Policy,* June 9, 2017.

[21] Republic of the Philippines, "Republic of the Philippines Bangsamoro Autonomous Region in Muslim Mindanao," webpage, undated; Stanford University, Center for International Security and Cooperation, 2019b.

and Lamitan.[22] The de facto capital of ARMM was Cotabato City, although it technically fell outside of ARMM's borders.

The ARMM solution was not enough to appease MNLF and MILF grievances, particularly as the MNLF purportedly was excluded from the negotiations. Sporadic conflict and negotiations with the government have continued; within Mindanao, the ARMM provinces have historically been the most heavily affected by conflict, with a 2013 study finding that Maguindanao and Basilan experienced the highest intensity of violence.[23] In March 2014, the Philippine government and the MILF signed a peace agreement called the Comprehensive Agreement on the Bangsamoro, proving the foundation for a power-sharing arrangement between the MILF and the Philippine government, called the Bangsamoro Basic Law (BBL) or the Bangsamoro Organic Law.[24] The BBL proposed the creation of the BARMM, which would replace the ARMM and better reflect the interests and concerns of the Muslim population in Mindanao.[25] Following attacks by the MILF and other extremist groups, Duterte delayed the implementation of the BBL, fueling further resentment and conflict and exacerbating tensions between various Muslim ethnic groups in the south and Christian groups in the north. The BBL was eventually ratified through referendums on January 21, 2019; on February 6, 2019, the BARMM officially replaced the ARMM.[26] The establishment of the BARMM did not end the violence; the peace process negotiations were punctuated by the suicide bombing attack on the cathedral on January 27, 2019.[27]

---

[22] Paul Hutchcroft, *Mindanao: The Long Journey to Peace and Prosperity*, Mandaluyong, Philippines: Anvil Publishing, 2016, p. 120.

[23] Abasolo, 2014, p. 5.

[24] International Crisis Group, *The Philippines: Renewing Prospects for Peace in Mindanao*, Brussels, Asia Report No. 281, July 6, 2016.

[25] International Crisis Group, 2016.

[26] John Unson, "ARMM Turns over Power to Bangsamoro Authority," *Philippine Star*, February 27, 2019.

[27] Michael Hart, "With Autonomy in the Philippines, Muslim Rebels Must Learn How to Govern," *World Politics Review*, February 12, 2019.

In a similar effort, Duterte initially sought to establish a truce with the CPP-NPA, proposing such concessions as releasing political prisoners and offering positions in his administration for individuals willing to join peace talks. He declared a ceasefire against the CPP-NPA and held formal peace talks between his administration and representatives of the Communist coalition in Norway in August 2016.[28] However, in July 2017, Duterte declared an end to negotiations because the NPA had attacked government forces in Mindanao.[29] In August 2017, the CPP-NPA announced that it would no longer cooperate with Duterte's administration and declared its intention to continue militant action—a promise it has kept by launching several attacks in the past few years.

Other Push Factors

Other push factors stem from circumstances at the individual level, such as mental illness, psychological disorders (such as depression or posttraumatic stress disorder), criminal behavior, or other personality traits that would make an individual more susceptible to radicalization.[30] Some studies have coded these factors as a category of their own,[31] but we believe they fall under the category of push factors, as they predispose or otherwise steer an individual toward radicalization.

Pull Factors

Terrorist and violent extremist groups in the Philippines actively recruit individuals through material incentives, in-person networks (i.e., friends, family, classmates, other personal connections), and online

---

[28] International Crisis Group, "Tracking Conflict Worldwide," webpage, undated.

[29] International Crisis Group, undated.

[30] Matteo Vergani, Muhammad Iqbal, Ekin Ilbahar, and Greg Barton, "The Three Ps of Radicalization: Push, Pull, and Personal. A Systematic Scoping Review of the Scientific Evidence About Radicalization into Violent Extremism," *Studies in Conflict and Terrorism*, 2018.

[31] See Vergani et al., 2018, for a systematic review of literature on personal factors.

propaganda. Others are drawn more organically to these groups by the idea that joining will give them power, camaraderie, and a sense of purpose. Some former combatants reported that the ability to avenge the death of friends or family members who died at the hands of the Philippine military or government played a major role in their radicalization.[32] In most groups, recruits are males from 15 to 30 years old.[33]

Material Incentives

Some groups have sought to attract young people by offering financial incentives or salaries ranging from 10,000 to 50,000 Philippine pesos (about \$200 to \$1,000).[34] Impoverished youth join these organizations as a means of providing for themselves and their families. In a recent study of the motivations of former members of the Maute Group, 15 of the 25 interviewees had joined because they were offered "a regular salary of between 20,000 and 50,000 pesos"; other material incentives, such as drugs, were a factor.[35] In addition, to entice potential recruits, ASG offers weapons and a monthly stipend to those willing to join the organization.

In-Person Networks

Both Communist and Islamist groups used to recruit heavily from schools and universities, but they have increasingly shifted to targeting uneducated youth and school dropouts, who might be more susceptible to radical ideologies.[36] Indeed, some extremist groups seek to draw uneducated young people in with the promise of providing them with an Islamic education; those with no moderate Islamic education have no basis for challenging radical teachings.[37] Some reports note

---

[32] Julie Chernov Hwang, "Relatives, Redemptions, and Rice: Motivations for Joining the Maute Group," *CTC Sentinel*, Vol. 12, No. 8, September 2019.

[33] Impl. Project, 2017b, slide 5.

[34] Samuel, 2016, p. 97.

[35] Hwang, 2019.

[36] Samuel, 2016, p. 98.

[37] Impl. Project, 2017a, slide 16.

that recruiters have been active in schools and mosques and that "most individuals gradually adopted radical views through listening to radical preachers, attending prayer groups, and having regular contact with the recruiters."[38] Some *madrasahs*—Islamic religious schools often attached to mosques—have served as fertile territory for recruitment, since they are subject to little government regulation and thus serve as a "major avenue for ideological indoctrination toward political extremism."[39]

Importantly, one study of radicalization drivers in Mindanao found that "family and social networks played a larger role in guiding radicalization and membership in armed groups than any specific grievances or social and economic factors did."[40] ASG has attracted foreign fighters from Southeast Asia, the Middle East, and North Africa. It relies on its members' families, friends, and other ties to the community for local support and recruitment, often sending its members into small villages to try to recruit people.[41] According to the study, although many factors contributed to the radicalization of individuals,

> [t]he pathways to extremism for many of the individuals profiled in western Mindanao began through family and social networks. Often, individuals became members of local armed groups focused on protecting their family and community from outsiders only to find themselves, knowingly or not, pulled into the orbit of more extreme groups. This finding also bears out in central Mindanao where social and family networks are key in guiding individuals toward extremism, and where being part of a small group of like-minded individuals provides a strong sense of community, particularly in the region's universities.[42]

---

[38] Institute for Autonomy and Governance, *Research on Youth Vulnerability to Violent Extremism in the Autonomous Region in Muslim Mindanao*, Cotabato City, Philippines, 2017, p. 2.

[39] Huesca, 2019, p. 60.

[40] Jessica Trisko Darden, *Tackling Terrorists' Exploitation of Youth*, Washington, D.C.: American Enterprise Institute, May 2019, p. 10.

[41] Roel Pareño, "Abu Sayyaf on Recruitment Spree," *Philstar Global*, January 21, 2016.

[42] Kevin Casey and David Pottebaum, *Youth and Violent Extremism in Mindanao, Philippines: A Mixed-Methods Design for Testing Assumptions About Drivers of Extremism*, Bethesda, Md.: DAI, August 24, 2018, p. 12.

Supporting this finding, in the aforementioned study of former members of the Maute Group, 15 of the 25 interviewees had been recruited by a friend or family member.[43]

Online Propaganda

Before the rise of ISIS-Philippines, ASG appears to have had the highest profile in the Philippines—at least in Mindanao, where a June 2017 survey of youth found that 70 percent of respondents were familiar with the ASG, 51 percent with ISIS, and fewer than 50 percent with other groups, such as the BIFF or Maute Group.[44] In terms of online efforts, the ASG largely relies on al Qaeda and ISIS to promote its message and does not proactively disseminate original content, although it has released a few propaganda videos on such platforms as YouTube. For instance, the 2007 film *The Filipino Lions Are Coming* contains scenes from ASG jungle training camps and archived speeches by Janjalani and his younger brother, who succeeded him.[45]

ASG fighters and supporters have also appeared in propaganda videos pledging allegiance to ISIS. In 2014, a group of ASG detainees released a video of themselves in a hall gathering around the ISIS flag and swearing allegiance to it. In a video released soon after, a group of men identifying themselves as ASG members also pledged allegiance to ISIS and Baghdadi.[46] A flag with the inscription "Soldiers of the Caliphate in the Philippines" has made appearances in several videos. The ASG has also released videos calling for Muslims to contribute to Filipino jihad, such as the 2011 video by Abu Jihad Khalil al-Rahman al-Luzoni, commander of an ASG-affiliated group.[47] This call to arms was repeated in 2016, when ISIS released a video encouraging its follow-

---

[43] Hwang, 2019.

[44] Institute for Autonomy and Governance, 2017, p. 1.

[45] Ian MacKinnon, "Philippine Islamists Post Fundraising Clip on YouTube," *The Guardian*, August 20, 2007.

[46] Soufan Group, "Islamic State Gains Traction in Southeast Asia," webpage, August 12, 2014.

[47] Robert Windrem, "ISIS Recruits Fighters for the Philippines Instead of Syria," *NBC News*, September 12, 2017.

ers in Southeast Asia to go to the Philippines rather than the Middle East if they wished to join the jihad.[48] The ASG does not maintain a website of its own, but videos and audio messages are promoted on al Qaeda–linked sites and the Shumukh al-Islam and Ansar al-Mujahideen English Forum, and ASG propaganda regularly appears on a Facebook page called Islamic Emirate of the Philippines: The Black Flag Movement. This page contains links to other extremist websites, including those run by al Qaeda and its proxies, and has blog-like radical posts, news updates, and photographs.[49] Some reports suggest that both the ASG and the Maute Group also used social media and other online outlets for recruitment, spreading propaganda, and fundraising, although there is no conclusive evidence of how effective these efforts have been.[50] These sites all propagate Islamist extremist narratives, drawing vulnerable people to join the associated terrorist organizations. Leveraging online recruitment has allowed these groups to recruit from outside their traditional sphere of influence in Mindanao.[51] These groups used social media to recruit combatants for the Marawi siege, attracting foreign fighters from various countries as well as recruits from across Mindanao.[52]

According to a study of extremist use of social media, social media provides groups with international reach, but, in practice, online interactions and networks in the Philippines typically mirror offline dynamics. This means that radicalization and recruitment often follows pathways that existed in the Philippines before social media exist-

---

[48] Camille Diola, "ISIS Releases First Propaganda Video for Philippines," *Philippine Star,* June 22, 2016.

[49] Rommel C. Banlaoi, "ISIS Threats and Followers in the Philippines," *Rappler,* August 5, 2014.

[50] Asia Foundation and Rappler, *Understanding Violent Extremism: Messaging and Recruitment Strategies on Social Media in the Philippines,* Pasig City, 2018, pp. 14, 20; Casey and Pottebaum, 2018, p. 2.

[51] Gilbert P. Felongco, "Terror Groups Taking Advantage of Cyberspace for Recruitment," *Gulf News Philippines,* April 27, 2017.

[52] Asia Foundation and Rappler, 2018, p. 5.

ed.[53] The study also found that most violent extremist interactions online are not strategically planned but rather are "opportunistic and unsophisticated."[54] Because of the localized nature of extremist social media, it remains difficult to detect and counter effectively (simply taking down publicly posted content will not prevent people from communicating privately within their established networks).[55]

ISIS-Philippines takes its recruitment and messaging cues from ISIS, preying on vulnerable populations and relying on glossy marketing materials to draw recruits to the organization.[56] As its self-proclaimed caliphate died in Iraq and Syria, ISIS has capitalized on the frustration of those who were unable to enter the Middle East, summoning would-be jihadists to join the fight in the Philippines instead.[57] ISIS has published several videos and social media posts specifically targeting Philippine citizens, particularly the more than 100,000 residents displaced after the Marawi siege.[58] In typical ISIS fashion, the organization has spun the government's failure to restore Marawi and adequately provide for its inhabitants to its narrative advantage, appealing to frustrated individuals with promises of a better life.[59] However, production of viral extremist social media content on ISIS channels slumped after the end of the battle of Marawi; those responsible for media outreach might have been killed or detained during the conflict, or ISIS might simply have moved away from these platforms.[60]

---

[53] Asia Foundation and Rappler, 2018, p. 5.

[54] Asia Foundation and Rappler, 2018, p. 5.

[55] Asia Foundation and Rappler, 2018, p. 5.

[56] Abuza and Clarke, 2019.

[57] Abuza and Clarke, 2019; Daniel L. Byman, "Frustrated Foreign Fighters," *Lawfare*, July 12, 2017.

[58] Bong S. Sarmiento, "ISIS Fading in Mid East, Thriving in the Philippines," *Asia Times*, October 30, 2019.

[59] Ted Regencia, "Delay in Return 'Boosts ISIL Recruitment' in Philippines' Marawi," *Al Jazeera*, October 22, 2019; Sarmiento, 2019.

[60] Asia Foundation and Rappler, 2018, p. 5.

Push Versus Pull Factors

Pull factors appear to be more powerful than push factors in the radicalization process. A systematic review of all radicalization-related literature (defined as all scholarly, peer-reviewed, English-language articles) published from 2001 to 2015 found that "pull factors are cited as a driver of radicalization in 78.4 percent of the articles ($n = 116$), push factors in 57.4 percent of the articles ($n = 85$), and personal factors in 39.2 percent of the articles ($n = 58$)."[61] This finding is not conclusive on its own and is not specific to the Philippines, but our review of the literature seems to support the idea that pull factors are more important than other factors in sparking radicalization. Although push factors can certainly amplify the effects of pull factors by creating vulnerability among individuals or groups, pull factors are more likely to be the decisive factor in setting an individual down the path to radicalization and violence. For example, an individual living in extreme poverty (a push factor), if left to his or her own devices, might not join a terrorist group to make a living unless the terrorist group was offering financial incentives (a pull factor). In addition, the pull of recruitment by friends and family members seems to trump push factors, such as ideology or specific grievances, when it comes to radicalization, even in cases where no other clear risk factors exist.

Ultimately, push and pull factors are so closely interrelated that it is difficult to parse their effects individually, but it is clear that the combined effects help motivate vulnerable populations to join terrorist or violent extremist groups.

---

[61] Vergani et al., 2018, p. 7.

CHAPTER THREE

Countering Violent Extremism Programs and Initiatives

Types of CVE Programs and Initiatives

The Philippines hosts CVE programs conducted by its own government, foreign governments, nongovernmental organizations (NGOs), and other organizations. The following sections provide an overview of the different types of CVE programs and initiatives, as well as the various implementing agencies.

Military and Policing Counterterrorism Responses

Since Duterte assumed office in June 2016, the Philippine government's response to terrorist and extremist groups has been largely characterized by tough military and policing approaches. Duterte declared martial law on the entire island of Mindanao in May 2017 and did not lift martial law until December 31, 2019.[1] The AFP serves as the country's major counterterrorism apparatus, with assistance from the PNP and special PNP units, such as the Anti-Kidnapping Group and Anti-Cybercrime Group. Under President Benigno Aquino III, there had been plans to transition more internal security functions, including domestic counterterrorism, to the PNP, but this transition has largely halted under Duterte because of his focus on an antidrug campaign.[2]

---

[1] Jason Gutierrez, "Duterte Says Martial Law in Southern Philippines Will End This Month," *New York Times*, December 10, 2019; "Philippines' Duterte to Lift Martial Law by Year's End," *Al Jazeera*, December 10, 2020.

[2] U.S. Department of State, 2018.

According to Duterte's Development Support and Security Plan Kapa-
yapaan, as announced in January 2017, the AFP's top priority is the
eradication of any terrorist groups operating within the Philippines.[3]
Simultaneously, the Philippine government has endeavored to increase
the role and improve the capabilities of the PNP in counterterrorism
and CVE efforts. The PNP's SAF—the tactical support unit that deals
with such situations as hostage crises and irregular warfare—boosted
its counterterrorism capabilities in May 2018 by forming five new battalions focused on urban warfare against rebel groups.[4] These counterterrorism efforts have complemented CVE efforts by serving as a
deterrent for would-be terrorists and degrading their capabilities. They
also have complicated CVE efforts by creating additional grievances
that can serve as drivers for radicalization.

Capacity-Building and Development Initiatives
Rather than seek to directly counter violent ideologies, many initiatives
in the Philippines are geared toward improving overall societal conditions and government capacity. Such activities might not be immedi-
ately recognizable as CVE efforts, but they contribute to CVE by elim-
inating or mitigating some of the most potent drivers of radicalization.

The Philippine government's primary CVE-related program is
Payapa at Masaganang Pamayanan (PAMANA), meaning "Resilient
Communities in Conflict-Affected Communities." PAMANA, which
is administered by the Office of the Presidential Advisor on the Peace
Process, aims to reduce push factors for radicalization by improving
governance on the national and local levels;[5] reducing poverty and
improving the delivery of social services; and empowering communities to mediate conflicts and broker peace by strengthening social cohesion. PAMANA focuses on conflict-affected, isolated, and vulnerable

---

[3] Amita Legaspi, "AFP Adopts New Security Plan Under Duterte," *GMA News Online*,
January 6, 2017.

[4] Maan Macapagal, "PNP-SAF Forms 5 New Battalions, Focuses on Urban Warfare Training," *ABS-CBN News*, May 9, 2018.

[5] Office of Presidential Adviser on the Peace Process, "Payapa at Masaganang Pamayanan
(PAMANA)," webpage, November 14, 2016.

areas, including many areas of Mindanao. PAMANA conducts activities at the national, community, and regional and subregional levels.[6] PAMANA has launched programs that provide protection for former rebels and their family members, as well as support to indigenous people and other marginalized groups.[7] For instance, one PAMANA initiative involved extending health insurance to nearly 4,000 former rebels from groups that are engaged in peace negotiations with the Philippine government.[8] Through such efforts, PAMANA seeks to ameliorate potential grievances and promote a sustainable peace.

The Philippines also has received capacity-building assistance from a variety of international organizations and governments. Recently, the U.S. Joint Special Operations Task Force–Philippines (JSOTF-P) has contributed to counterterrorism and CVE operations by providing "training, advice, and assistance to conventional AFP units at all echelons throughout Mindanao, including Philippine Army, Marine Corps, Navy, and Air Force units . . . [and] the PNP Special Action Forces."[9] The United States ended JSOTF-P activities in June 2015 but retained some personnel in the Philippines in an advisory capacity. After the U.S. special operations forces (SOF) initiative ended, SOF personnel "judged that Philippine SOF [were] among the most proficient of those Asian SOF units with which they had worked."[10] In addition, the U.S. Department of State's Antiterrorism Assistance program has provided training and equipment to the PNP-SAF and other units involved in counterterrorism or CVE efforts. In 2015, the U.S. Department of State also helped the Philippines establish a Combined Special Outreach Group, which is a "joint AFP-PNP effort to share best practices and combine strategies for public messaging on peace and order

---

[6] Office of Presidential Adviser on the Peace Process, 2016.

[7] Counter Extremism Project, undated b, p. 8.

[8] Counter Extremism Project, undated b, p. 8.

[9] U.S. Senate, *U.S. Government Efforts to Counter Violent Extremism*, Washington, D.C.: U.S. Government Printing Office, 2010, p. 60; Linda Robinson, Patrick B. Johnston, and Gillian S. Oak, *U.S. Special Operations Forces in the Philippines, 2001–2014*, Santa Monica, Calif.: RAND Corporation, RR-1236-OSD, 2016, p. xiv.

[10] Robinson, Johnston, and Oak, 2016, p. xiv.

and CVE outreach" to "improve outreach and messaging in communities vulnerable to radicalization to violence."[11] Through the Combined Special Outreach Group, the Philippine government has also worked with U.S. Pacific Command's Military Information Support Team.[12]

Other U.S.-driven initiatives include efforts by USAID, which has worked with local institutions and civil society organizations to implement a variety of capacity-building initiatives to improve governance, delivery of health and social services, access to and quality of education, and other socioeconomic conditions.[13] USAID has also worked with religious and community leaders to help broker peace between rival factions to reduce violent conflicts over land, resources, and other disputes.[14] In a similar vein, another international development initiative, the Impl. Project, surveyed individuals in four provinces in Mindanao (Lanao del Norte, Lanao del Sur, Maguindanao, and Sultan Kudarat) to identify local grievances and drivers of instability and "facilitate community-driven development programming" tailored to address issues raised by locals.[15]

Australia has provided support to CVE programs, particularly those that adopt a development or peace-building approach, in the Philippines. In March 2018, Australia offered to help the Philippine government improve the PNP's counterterrorism capabilities and to aid reconstruction efforts in Marawi City.[16] Australia has signed onto Association of Southeast Asian Nations (ASEAN) agreements to cooperate with other countries in the region on CVE efforts.[17] Australia also conducts a program called Building Sustainable Institutions and

---

[11] U.S. Department of State, "Building a Global Movement to Address Violent Extremism," fact sheet, September 2015.

[12] AFP Information Support Affairs, "CVE/Counter Narrative Efforts," briefing, undated, slide 10.

[13] Asia Foundation, 2013, p. 2.

[14] USAID, 2018.

[15] Impl. Project, 2017b, slide 2.

[16] "Australia Backs Philippine Campaign Against Terrorism," *Straits Times*, March 19, 2018.

[17] "Australia Backs Philippine Campaign Against Terrorism," 2018.

Communities in Bangsamoro, through which it has provided technical assistance and support for the peace process in Mindanao.[18]

A variety of international organizations have provided CVE-related capability training to Philippine agencies. For example, the International Centre for Counter-Terrorism in the Hague has trained Philippine experts on rehabilitation and reintegration of violent extremist actors.[19] The United Nations Office on Drugs and Crime and the Anti-Money Laundering Council Secretariat have trained Filipino counterterrorism officials on counterterrorist financing skills.[20]

Regional and International Cooperation on CVE

Some terrorist groups operate beyond national borders—particularly in the maritime region of Southeast Asia—and several Asian countries have sought to jointly address their violent extremism issues. As a member of ASEAN, the Philippines has adopted the ASEAN Regional Forum Work Plan for Counter Terrorism and Transnational Crime, which identifies the prevention of violent extremism as one of its five priorities.[21] In April 2015, the Philippines also adopted the Langkawi Declaration on the Global Movement of Moderates, in which ASEAN signatories agreed to conduct activities to promote moderate, democratic values—such as interfaith dialogues, educational initiatives, and training programs—and enhance cooperation within ASEAN-led agencies involved in CVE.[22] The Philippines also participates in the annual Multilateral CVE Working Group, which includes representatives from several ASEAN countries and "provides a forum for regional partners to build relationships across regional security seams, hold discussions about radicalization, and develop collaborative solu-

---

[18] Australian Government, Department of Foreign Affairs and Trade, *Australia's Support for Peace in Mindanao: Strategic Review and Management Response*, Canberra, undated.

[19] U.S. Department of State, 2018.

[20] Asia Foundation, 2013, p. 2.

[21] Republic of the Philippines Department of Foreign Affairs, "Philippines Co-Hosts Workshop on Mainstreaming the Prevention of Violent Extremism in the ARF Region in Brussels," press release, February 27, 2017.

[22] Counter Extremism Project, undated b, p. 9.

tions to counter and prevent violent extremism."[23] In a similar vein, the Philippines has also hosted a number of international workshops and conferences, such as the Countering Violent Extremism in Southeast Asia workshop in Manila in March 2018.[24] The Philippines is also a member of the Asia Pacific Group on Money Laundering, and it continues to work with the organization to address persistent issues with money laundering and terrorist financing.[25]

In an effort to reduce the incidence of kidnappings and attacks at sea by Islamist extremists, the Philippines struck a May 2016 agreement with Indonesia and Malaysia to coordinate policing of Southeast Asian shipping lanes.[26] The Philippines also has participated in Interpol's Border Management Program, the U.S. Department of State's Airport Security Management training courses, and the U.S. Coast Guard's International Port Security Program.[27] The Philippine Navy, Coast Guard, and PNP also have been strengthening their capabilities to provide maritime security and investigate cases. In early 2018, the Philippines and Indonesia agreed to focus on providing increased access to education to Muslim youth across Southeast Asia as a CVE measure.[28]

Community Engagement and Educational Initiatives

Several activities conducted by various organizations aim to promote dialogue and cooperation between Muslims and Christian communities and to educate the general public on CVE issues. Such interfaith groups include the Peacemaker's Circle Foundation, Religions for Peace Philippines, and the Bishop-Ulama Conference. The Bishop-

---

[23] U.S. Indo-Pacific Command, "Pacific Special Operations Forces Sponsor Countering Violent Extremism Workshop in Guam," press release, Camp H. M. Smith, Hawaii, May 31, 2017.

[24] Daniel K. Inouye Asia-Pacific Center for Security Studies, "Workshop Brings Together CVE Experts in Southeast Asia," webpage, March 26, 2018.

[25] Counter Extremism Project, undated b, p. 9.

[26] Counter Extremism Project, undated b, p. 9.

[27] U.S. Department of State, 2018.

[28] Christina Mendez and Pia Lee-Brago, "Duterte, Indonesian Envoy Vow Closer Bilateral Cooperation," *Philippine Star,* January 5, 2018.

Ulama Conference was launched in 1996. It is made up of Catholic, Protestant, and Muslim leaders; official observers from a confederation (the *Panagtagbo*) of the indigenous peoples of Mindanao; and a board of directors, called the Tripartite Commission.[29] To better relations and foster discussion between the Moro minority and the Christian majority, the Bishop-Ulama Conference hosts triannual meetings with support from the National Secretariat for Social Action, Justice and Peace, the Office of the Presidential Adviser on the Peace Process, and Catholic Relief Services.[30]

The U.S. embassy has also spearheaded the Youth Council Summit and has hosted two *iftars* (the meal eaten by Muslims after sunset during the holiday of Ramadan), which brought together many religious leaders, Muslim youth, civil society organizations, and local officials.[31] In addition, the U.S. embassy's Mindanao Working Group facilitates interfaith dialogue among religious and community leaders. The Philippine government has encouraged Muslim religious leaders to participate in policy debates through such organizations as the Philippine Center for Islam and Democracy and the National Ulama Council of the Philippines.[32]

The Asia Foundation, in conjunction with USAID, runs a program called Transforming Conflicts in Sulu and Basilan through People-to-People Engagement, which aims to "reduce localized violence by transforming social relationships and establishing effective linkages among the influential members of rival groups in conflict-affected areas of the Sulu Archipelago."[33] The program focuses on facilitating dialogue and engagement between Muslim and Christian leaders and develops the capacity of these leaders—especially women leaders—to

---

[29] Peace Direct, "The Bishop-Ulama Conference (BUC)," webpage, last updated December 2015.

[30] Peace Direct, 2015.

[31] U.S. Department of State, Bureau of Democracy, Human Rights and Labor, 2013, p. 6.

[32] Asia Foundation, 2013, p. 4.

[33] Asia Foundation, 2013, p. 2.

mediate conflicts and promote peace.[34] Examples of specific activities include the interfaith Culture of Peace Festival held in 2013, the Sulu Provincial Women's Council Planning Workshops, and the Dialogue Between Muslim and Christian Youth Leaders.[35]

The AFP's Civil Military Operations Group (AFP-CMO) and Information Development Group also run programs focused on community engagement, education about CVE, stakeholder engagement, and counter-radicalization.[36] As part of the community engagement program, the AFP-CMO provides families with the opportunity to learn about CVE; enables local actors to deliver interventions to individuals and communities to make them less vulnerable to extremist influence; and connects with youth by organizing a youth leadership summit, as well as sports and arts activities.[37] The AFP-CMO's other education efforts include raising community awareness of violent extremism issues and how best to identify and counter them, providing a forum to discuss CVE issues, soliciting suggestions for solutions from the community, and offering information on CVE through its own training curriculum.[38] In addition, the AFP established a text hotline that allows people to report suspected cases of radicalization, and the PNP-SAF runs a counter-radicalization program at several universities.[39]

Another important initiative conducted by Equal Access International (EAI) are tech camps, which are intensive programs (typically about one week in length) that train selected local influencers (primarily youth) on ways to use social media and other technology to counter extremist narratives and promote peaceful content. Some participants were selected for peace promotion fellowships, which allowed them to design and implement their own CVE projects in their respec-

---

[34] Asia Foundation, 2013, p. 2.

[35] Asia Foundation, 2013, p. 2.

[36] AFP Information Support Affairs, undated, slides 3–9.

[37] AFP Information Support Affairs, undated, slides 6–9.

[38] AFP Information Support Affairs, undated, slides 6–9.

[39] AFP Information Support Affairs, undated, slide 38; Philippine National Police, *Annual Report 2016*, Quezon City, undated.

tive communities.[40] Finally, in 2019 and 2020, EAI held peace summits in Mindanao that convened hundreds of individuals from the peacebuilding community, youth organizations, academia, local and national government, and NGOs.[41]

Deradicalization and Rehabilitation in Prisons

As in many other countries, prison radicalization is a source of concern in the Philippines. For instance, New Bilibid Prison is a maximum security prison that holds inmates from the ASG and the BIFF; it is severely overcrowded at 165 percent capacity.[42] The close proximity of masses of discontented, radicalized individuals to the general prison population has raised concerns that more inmates will become radicalized and those that are already radicalized will become more radical. The Bureau of Jail Management and Penology runs counter-radicalization programs in facilities where ASG members and other terrorism suspects are held pending trial.[43] The bureau released a training manual titled *Operational Guidelines on Inmate Classification and Counseling Unit*.[44] In addition, the Global Counterterrorism Forum assisted the Philippine government in applying the *Rome Memorandum on Good Practices for Rehabilitation and Reintegration of Violent Extremism Offenders* and sponsored the Workshop on Developing Effective

---

[40] Ashley L. Rhoades, Todd C. Helmus, James V. Marrone, Victoria M. Smith, and Elizabeth Bodine-Baron, *Promoting Peace as the Antidote to Violent Extremism: Evaluation of a Philippines-Based Tech Camp Training and Peace Promotion Fellowship*, Santa Monica, Calif.: RAND Corporation, RR-A233-3, 2020.

[41] EAI, "Updated Post! OURmindaNOW Summit 2020 in Mindanao, Philippines," webpage, undated b.

[42] Arie W. Kruglanski, Michele J. Gelfand, Anna Shreveland, Maxim Babush, Malkanthi Hetiarachchi, Michele Ng Bonto, and Rohan Gunaratna, "What a Difference Two Years Make: Patterns of Radicalization in a Philippine Jail," *Dynamics of Asymmetric Conflict*, Vol. 9, Nos. 1–3, 2016, p. 15.

[43] Clarke R. Jones and Resurrecion S. Morales, "Integration Versus Segregation: A Preliminary Examination of Philippine Correctional Facilities for De-Radicalization," *Studies in Conflict and Terrorism*, Vol. 35, No. 3, 2012.

[44] U.S. Department of State, 2018.

Intake, Risk Assessment, and Monitoring Tools and Strategies for Incarcerated Terrorist Offenders.[45]

Legal Measures and Authorities

The Philippines has passed several pieces of legislation strengthening various aspects of its counterterrorism capabilities. The primary CVE-related legislation in the Philippines is Republic Act No. 9372 of 2007, titled An Act to Secure the State and Protect Our People from Terrorism.[46] The act criminalizes and defines terrorism and other relevant terms, stipulates regulations for surveillance, and includes provisions for countering terrorist financing efforts.[47] The act also establishes the Anti-Terrorism Council (ATC) to oversee general implementation of the law and the National Counter-Terrorism Action Group, under the ATC, that is responsible for "the actual investigation and evidence-finding for prosecutors in the event of a terrorist attack."[48] The Office of the United Nations High Commissioner for Human Rights has expressed concerns about the law, claiming that it might provide a basis for infringing on human rights and compromise rule of law.[49] In April 2016, the ATC

> facilitated a national consultation on CVE, producing a set of recommendations to formulate a National Action Plan to Prevent and Counter Violent Extremism. The Duterte administration has not released the National Action Plan, but cooperated with international partners and organizations to refine and improve CVE strategies.[50]

---

[45] U.S. Department of State, *Country Reports on Terrorism 2016*, Washington, D.C., 2016.

[46] Republic of the Philippines, Republic Act No. 9372, An Act to Secure the State and Protect Our People from Terrorism, 2007.

[47] Republic of the Philippines, 2007.

[48] Counter Extremism Project, undated b, p. 7.

[49] United Nations Office of the High Commissioner for Human Rights, "UN Special Rapporteur Calls for Changes to the Philippines' Human Security Act," press release, March 12, 2007.

[50] U.S. Department of State, 2018.

More-recent legislation has bolstered various aspects of the 2007 act. These include 2012's Republic Act No. 10168, The Terrorism Financing Prevention and Suppression Act, which made terrorist financing an independent crime, and Republic Act No. 10365, which expanded the Anti-Money Laundering Act of 2001 to include terrorist financing.[51] Internationally, the Philippines cosponsored United Nations Security Council Resolution 2178 on Foreign Terrorist Fighters, which included several measures to try to combat the foreign fighter threat.[52] In December 2016, the Philippines applied sanctions against ISIS and al Qaeda, as called for by the United Nations Security Council.

Online and Countermessaging Campaigns

Several Filipino universities have participated in the Facebook Global Digital Challenge as part of EdVenture Partner's Peer to Peer program.[53] One of the most high-profile campaigns that emerged from this initiative was Xavier University's I Am Mindanao campaign, which targets college students and aims to educate them about violent extremism and reduce their susceptibility to radicalization by "strengthening their sense of identity, belonging, and purpose."[54] The campaign has reached an estimated 5.2 million people through online content, such as short documentary films about conflict in Mindanao. Connecting the online campaign to real-life initiatives, the team also holds an I Am Mindanao Peace Camp to foster dialogue and understanding between Muslim and Christian youth, as well as seminars and workshops on peace building.[55] I Am Mindanao has a related campaign, PeaceKwela, which conducts similar activities but targets a younger demographic

---

[51] Counter Extremism Project, undated b, p. 5.

[52] United Nations Security Council, Resolution 2178, September 24, 2014.

[53] Stephan J. Pedroza, "'I Am Mindanao' Campaign Among Final Four in Digital Challenge," Republic of the Philippines Philippine Information Agency, July 3, 2017b.

[54] I Am Mindanao, homepage, undated.

[55] Stephen J. Pedroza, "I Am Mindanao Campaign Goes Global," Xavier University, press release, June 30, 2017a.

of junior high school students. I Am Mindanao runs a website, a blog, and Facebook, Twitter, and Instagram accounts.

In response to the battle in Marawi, the AFP produced material to counter the Maute Group's narrative, including audiovisual presentations, hundreds of articles, 24/7 news coverage of the Marawi conflict, and brochures containing information about wanted terrorists.[56] The AFP also monitored and subsequently removed more than 100 Maute Group sympathizer accounts on Facebook.[57] The AFP and local NGOs also launched the *#OgopMarawi* ("Help Marawi") campaign in June 2017. This campaign aimed to provide aid to the people displaced by the conflict in Marawi and boost the morale of soldiers stationed in Marawi."[58] The AFP's social media efforts have reportedly reached more than 28 million people.[59]

Another significant countermessaging campaign is EAI's Alternative Messaging Hubs initiative, which seeks to strengthen "capacities of local organizations to build resilience to violent extremism and counter the ideologies and recruitment efforts of armed groups in Mindanao."[60] The Alternative Messaging Hub model encompasses several activities, such as social media campaigns, stakeholder workshops, and radio programs providing positive messaging to counteract extremist narratives. *Sarrangola*, a radio drama that promotes youth and women's empowerment and good governance, is a major component of the Alternative Messaging Hub; it is specifically designed for vulnerable audiences in Mindanao.

Other radio programs conducted by different organizations have also contributed to peacebuilding initiatives in Mindanao. For instance, *Radio Gandingan*, a program by the Notre Dame Broadcasting Corporation that has been broadcasting since 2000 and still airs multiple

---

[56] AFP Information Support Affairs, undated, slide 25.

[57] AFP Information Support Affairs, undated, slide 25.

[58] Philippine Embassy in Washington DC, USA, "#OgopMarawi (Help Marawi)," Facebook post, June 30, 2017.

[59] AFP Information Support Affairs, undated, slide 25.

[60] EAI, "OURmindaNOW: Alternative Messaging Hub in Mindanao, Philippines," webpage, undated a.

times a week, focuses on providing content to promote peace among "minority Maguindanaon communities severely affected by decades of armed struggle for political autonomy involving multiple state, civil, political, religious, and armed actors."[61] During the battle of Marawi, *Radio Gandingan* provided updates on the conflict and helpful information from the government, particularly for evacuees. [62]

Lessons for CVE Efforts in the Philippines

We have identified a variety of ways to improve CVE policies and programming in the Philippines. In this section, we suggest some best practices for future program design and implementation. Most critiques of CVE efforts focus on government programs, as these have received a great deal of media attention and have sometimes been counterproductive because of indiscriminate or overly aggressive use of violence. Moreover, government CVE efforts tend to be the best documented and the most studied; it is difficult to find information on other efforts. Therefore, we have divided our suggestions for areas of improvement and best practices into those that apply to government programs and those that apply to NGO programs. Because these recommendations are based solely on our review of the literature and current CVE efforts, we do not present these as comprehensive or definitive findings; rather, we hope this information will provide implementers with helpful ideas. Future research and rigorous evaluation of CVE programming could build on and significantly supplement these rudimentary findings.

Lessons for Government-Implemented CVE Programs

The literature offers several recommendations for the Philippine government to improve its approach to CVE and other terrorist-prevention programs. Poor interagency coordination, lack of information sharing,

---

[61] Ross W. James, Ella Romo-Murphy, and Mae-Mosette Oczon-Quirante, "A Realist Evaluation of a Community-Centered Radio Initiative for Health and Development in Mindanao, Philippines," *Asia Pacific Journal of Public Health*, Vol. 31, No. 6, 2019.

[62] James, Romo-Murphy, and Oczon-Quirante, 2019.

and unclear divisions of responsibilities lead to duplicative or conflicting efforts when multiple agencies are engaged in counterterrorism and CVE efforts, as they are in the Philippines. Coordination between the AFP and the PNP has recently improved, but it remains problematic.[63] In addition, Philippine legal and judicial capacity remains limited, resulting in a low number of terrorism-related prosecutions.[64] Because of high levels of corruption, municipal and barangay (the smallest administrative division) officials rarely use funds for their intended purposes, and many institutions never receive the services or assistance they need. For instance, the National Commission on Muslim Filipinos, a moderate Muslim organization, has been waiting months for government funds.[65]

Moreover, as with efforts in other countries, the Philippine government's intense counterterrorism campaign has prompted criticism that its police and military operations unnecessarily alienate local Mindanao populations and potentially contribute to radicalization.[66] The International Crisis Group argued that the Philippine government should work to reduce civilian casualties either by evacuating them during adjacent military operations or otherwise limiting collateral damage from kinetic operations.[67] This would entail limiting airstrikes and the use of artillery and standoff weapons.[68]

The Philippine government should continue providing increased security through checkpoints and arms control initiatives, as these have yielded positive results and have been largely met with approval. The International Crisis Group report found that there were "fewer violent incidents in absolute numbers in 2017 than 2016, attributable in large measure to martial law and stricter enforcement of reg-

---

[63] U.S. Department of State, 2018.

[64] U.S. Department of State, 2018.

[65] Impl. Project, 2017a, slide 16.

[66] U.S. Department of State, 2018.

[67] International Crisis Group, 2019, p. 25.

[68] International Crisis Group, 2019, p. 25.

ulations on firearms."[69] Complete disarmament of militant groups is unlikely in practice, but the Philippine government could work with the new Bangsamoro government to establish formal or informal local-level agreements on weapons regulation to facilitate demilitarization efforts.[70] In particular, national and local government officials should ensure that there are programs and resources in place to

> enable MILF fighters to return to civilian life. [As] programs providing training and helping former combatants and their families find new livelihoods will be essential to mitigate the risk of creating a new recruitment pool for armed groups including militants.[71]

The Bangsamoro Transitional Authority has a narrow window of opportunity in which it can "reap a peace dividend," and the new Bangsamoro government should act quickly to prove that it is capable of delivering on its promises before the population becomes disillusioned.[72] The new Bangsamoro government should focus on rebuilding Marawi, restoring displaced people to their homes, and delivering important goods and services, such as education, health, and other infrastructure. Extremist groups themselves, particularly the MILF and the BIFF, could play a role in peacebuilding efforts. In particular, the MILF could help broker lasting peace and assert itself as a legitimate authority within the new Bangsamoro government by addressing the concerns of area residents who did not wish to join the BARMM but are now a part of the region.[73]

Lessons for Nongovernmental CVE Programming
CVE efforts around the globe would benefit from more-independent and rigorous evaluations to inform program priorities and design, iden-

---

[69] International Crisis Group, 2019, p. 25.

[70] International Crisis Group, 2019, p. 26.

[71] International Crisis Group, 2019, p. 27.

[72] International Crisis Group, 2019, p. 25.

[73] International Crisis Group, 2019, p. 25.

tify areas for improvement in program implementation, and measure the impact of completed and ongoing programs. Few such evaluations of CVE programming in the Philippines have been conducted, although many organizations conduct informal assessments of their own programming.[74] A review of these assessments and the wide array of CVE initiatives currently underway in the Philippines provide some general impressions of successful practices.

One approach that seems successful is community-centered engagement. For instance, *Radio Gandingan* reportedly allowed community participation and a sense of ownership by "facilitat[ing] dialogue, which strengthened community cohesion, opened lines of communication between community leaders and their constituents, and resolved conflict through resolution models introduced in programming content, particularly drama."[75]

Another important best practice of CVE programs is the inclusion of youth as program leaders. Because youth are particularly vulnerable to radicalization and recruitment efforts, giving them agency and equipping them with the skills to promote resiliency among their networks is important. As one study noted,

> [w]ith so much energy, idealism, and enthusiasm, [youth] are particularly useful in Track II diplomatic strategies such as interfaith dialog[ue], community-based conflict resolution, peace education and advocacy, [and] socioeconomic empowerment.[76]

The United Nations Security Council adopted Resolution 2250 on December 9, 2015, urging member states to find ways of engag-

---

[74] For example, RAND researchers conducted a process evaluation of EAI's tech camp and Peace Promotion Fellowship programs. After interviewing participants in the program and analyzing surveys, the researchers offered a number of recommendations for program improvement. The researchers also attempted a randomized control trial evaluation of an EAI radio program. Unfortunately, various problems afflicted the integrity of the data, and the study results could not be finalized (Rhoades et al., 2020).

[75] James, Romo-Murphy, and Oczon-Quirante, 2019, p. 568.

[76] Huesca, 2019, p. 64.

ing youth in peace processes.[77] Most ongoing CVE programs in the Philippines already involve youth to some degree, and there have been many success stories resulting from these efforts. For example, the NGO Kapamagogopa Incorporated has focused on "mobilizing youth toward peace and development initiatives in Muslim and non-Muslim communities across Mindanao," executing the Muslim Youth Volunteering for Peace and Development program and the Interfaith Youth Dialogue.[78] Another youth organization, United Youth for Peace and Development, worked with the Asia Foundation and USAID to broker a resolution to a protracted conflict between two feuding clans in Mindanao in 2007.[79]

Program designers should use evaluative tools to direct CVE efforts to the areas where they are most needed. The International Alert UK Philippines Program established a Violence Intensity Index as part of the Bangsamoro Conflict Monitoring System. This index allows CVE implementers to pinpoint areas that are most affected by violence and conflict.[80] Because the drivers of radicalization are not always clear and shift over time, development funds may work best when "directed at small-scale projects that improve the quality of local government services, thereby inducing noncombatants to share intelligence about insurgents with their government and its allies."[81] Drawing on CVE experiences in other countries, the Philippine government should also be wary of implementing programs that seek to override Muslim ideologies with a "state-supported brand of Islam"; doing so could intensify tensions between Muslim and Christian communities and further alienate Filipino Muslims.[82]

---

[77] Huesca, 2019, p. 58.

[78] Huesca, 2019, p. 63.

[79] Huesca, 2019, p. 63.

[80] Abasolo, 2014.

[81] Berman et al., 2011, p. 519.

[82] Joseph Franco, "Preventing Other 'Marawis' in the Southern Philippines," *Asia and the Pacific Policy Studies*, Vol. 5, No. 2, 2018.

Conclusion

CVE initiatives in the Philippines must address endemic drivers of radicalization and the evolving threat posed by myriad militant extremist groups. Our review of the literature on existing terrorist groups and drivers of radicalization indicates that the threat of terrorism and violent extremism in the Philippines is severe and persistent, as current conditions—such as extreme poverty in areas of the Philippines, divisions between Catholic and Muslim culture and communities, grievances with the government, and recurring conflict—create a ripe environment for violent ideology to be planted and take root. Moreover, current programming is insufficient to mitigate the threat. Government responses, particularly under Duterte, have been far too heavy-handed, prompting further radicalization among frustrated and desperate individuals. Beyond kinetic counterterrorism efforts, government programming in the CVE space also has suffered from a perceived lack of credibility, limited judicial capacity, and poor coordination. Although some nongovernmental CVE programming in the Philippines has proven successful, these programs are often microcampaigns and have not had a wide-scale impact. Existing programming is also plagued by a lack of systematic, rigorous evaluation, making it difficult to gauge progress, effects, and areas that need improvement. Future CVE efforts should make a concerted effort to monitor and evaluate programs during implementation. Doing so will mitigate at least one challenge in the exceedingly difficult fight against the scourge of violent extremism in the Philippines.

References

Abasolo, Ever J., *Applying a Violence Intensity Index in the Bangsamoro*, London: International Alert, 2014.

Abuza, Zachary, "Duterte Thinks He Can Bomb Islamists into Submission. He Cannot," *New York Times*, June 21, 2017.

Abuza, Zachary, and Colin P. Clarke, "The Islamic State Meets Southeast Asia," *Foreign Affairs*, September 16, 2019. As of August 7, 2020:
https://www.foreignaffairs.com/articles/southeast-asia/2019-09-16/islamic-state-meets-southeast-asia

AFP Information Support Affairs—*See* Armed Forces of the Philippines Information Support Affairs.

Armed Forces of the Philippines Information Support Affairs, "CVE/Counter Narrative Efforts," briefing, undated.

Asia Foundation, *Transforming Conflicts in Sulu and Basilan Through People-to-People Engagement*, Makati City, Philippines, 2013.

Asia Foundation and Rappler, *Understanding Violent Extremism: Messaging and Recruitment Strategies on Social Media in the Philippines*, Pasig City, 2018. As of August 7, 2020:
https://asiafoundation.org/wp-content/uploads/2019/02/Understanding-Violent-Extremism-Messaging-and-Recruitment-on-Social-Media-in-the-Philippines.pdf

"Australia Backs Philippine Campaign Against Terrorism," *Straits Times*, March 19, 2018. As of July 18, 2018:
https://www.straitstimes.com/asia/se-asia/australia-backs-philippine-campaign-against-terrorism

Australian Government, Department of Foreign Affairs and Trade, *Australia's Support for Peace in Mindanao: Strategic Review and Management Response*, Canberra, undated. As of July 18, 2018:
https://www.dfat.gov.au/sites/default/files/strategic-review-australias-support-for-peace-in-mindanao.pdf

Banlaoi, Rommel C., "Current Terrorist Groups and Emerging Extremist Armed Movements in the Southern Philippines," in Fermin R. De Leon, Jr., and Ernesto R. Aradanas, *National Security Review, The Study of National Security at 50: Reawakenings*, Quezon City: National Defense College of the Philippines, 2013, pp. 163–180. As of August 12, 2020:
http://www.ndcp.edu.ph/wp-content/uploads/publications/BANLAOI_ Current%20Terrorist%20Groups%20and%20Emerging%20Extremist%20 Armed%20Movement%20in%20the%20Southern%20Philippines%20 Threats%20to%20Philippine%20National%20Security.pdf

———,"ISIS Threats and Followers in the Philippines," *Rappler*, August 4, 2014. As of August 7, 2020:
https://rappler.com/voices/thought-leaders/isis-threats-followers-philippines

Beech, Hannah, and Jason Gutierrez, "How ISIS Is Rising in the Philippines as It Dwindles in the Middle East," *New York Times*, March 12, 2019. As of August 7, 2020:
https://www.nytimes.com/2019/03/09/world/asia/isis-philippines-jolo.html

Berman, Eli, Michael Callan, Joseph H. Felter, and Jacob N. Shapiro, "Do Working Men Rebel? Insurgency and Unemployment in Afghanistan, Iraq, and the Philippines," *Journal of Conflict Resolution*, Vol. 55, No. 4, 2011.

Byman, Daniel L., "Frustrated Foreign Fighters," *Lawfare*, July 12, 2017. As of August 7, 2020:
https://www.lawfareblog.com/frustrated-foreign-fighters

Cahiles, Gerg, "Expert Doubts MILF Combatants Will Disarm Completely," *CNN Philippines*, June 17, 2015. As of August 7, 2020:
https://cnnphilippines.com/regional/2015/06/17/ Expert-doubts-MILF-combatants-will-disarm-completely.html1

Capuno, Joseph J., "Probing Conflict Contagion and Casualties in Mindanao, Philippines, Defence and Peace Economics," *Defense and Peace Economics*, 2019.

Casey, Kevin, and David Pottebaum, *Youth and Violent Extremism in Mindanao, Philippines: A Mixed-Methods Design for Testing Assumptions About Drivers of Extremism*, Bethesda, Md.: DAI, August 24, 2018. As of August 15, 2020:
https://www.dai.com/uploads/Youth%20and%20Violent%20Extremism%20 in%20Mindanao,%20Philippines.pdf

Chase-Lubitz, Jesse, "Duterte's War on Terror Also Looks Like a War on Civilians," *Foreign Policy*, June 9, 2017. As of August 7, 2020:
https://foreignpolicy.com/2017/06/09/ dutertes-war-on-terror-also-looks-like-a-war-on-civilians/

Cibulka, Frank, "The Philippines: In the Eye of the Political Storm," in Daljit Singh and Lorraine C. Salazar, eds., *Southeast Asian Affairs 2007*, Singapore: Institute of Southeast Asian Affairs, 2007, pp. 257–276.

Cockburn, Harry, "Philippines: Muslims 'Being Profiled' Under Martial Law," *The Independent*, August 20, 2017. As of July 18, 2018: https://www.independent.co.uk/news/world/asia/muslims-being-profiled-martial-law-philippines-president-rodrigo-duterte-a7903761.html

Counter Extremism Project, "Abu Sayyaf Group (ASG)," webpage, undated a. As of July 18, 2018: https://www.counterextremism.com/threat/abu-sayyaf-group-asg

———, *The Philippines: Extremism and Counter-Extremism*, New York, undated b. As of July 18, 2018: https://www.counterextremism.com/countries/philippines

Craun, Sarah W., Mark J. Rossin, and Matthew R. Collier, "Interpretations of Proof-of-Life Videos and Their Impact on Supported Interventions," *Journal of Policing, Intelligence and Counter Terrorism*, Vol. 14, No. 2, 2019, pp. 115–128.

Dancel, Raul, "Marawi a Crucible of Filipino Identity," *Straits Times*, January 18, 2018. As of July 18, 2018: https://www.straitstimes.com/opinion/marawi-a-crucible-of-filipino-identity

Daniel K. Inouye Asia-Pacific Center for Security Studies, "Workshop Brings Together CVE Experts in Southeast Asia," webpage, March 26, 2018. As of July 18, 2018: https://apcss.org/workshop-brings-together-cve-experts-in-southeast-asia

Darden, Jessica Trisko, *Tackling Terrorists' Exploitation of Youth*, Washington, D.C.: American Enterprise Institute, May 2019. As of August 7, 2020: https://www.un.org/sexualviolenceinconflict/wp-content/uploads/2019/05/report/tackling-terrorists-exploitation-of-youth/Tackling-Terrorists-Exploitation-of-Youth.pdf

Diola, Camille, "ISIS Releases First Propaganda Video for Philippines," *Philippine Star*, June 22, 2016. As of August 15, 2020: https://www.philstar.com/headlines/2016/06/22/1595580/isis-releases-first-propaganda-video-philippines

Dunham-Scott, Diana, *Understanding and Engaging the Muslims of the Southern Philippines*, dissertation, Pardee RAND Graduate School, Santa Monica, Calif.: RAND Corporation, RGSD-301, 2012. As of July 20, 2020: https://www.rand.org/pubs/rgs_dissertations/RGSD301.html

EAI—*See* Equal Access International.

Ellis-Petersen, Hannah, and Carmela Fonbuena, "Philippines: Scores of Islamic State Fighters on Mindanao Island," *The Guardian*, November 11, 2018. As of August 7, 2020: https://www.theguardian.com/world/2018/nov/11/philippines-scores-of-islamic-state-fighters-on-mindanao-island

Equal Access International, "OURmindaNOW: Alternative Messaging Hub in Mindanao, Philippines," webpage, undated a. As of August 7, 2020:
https://www.equalaccess.org/our-work/projects/
alternative-messaging-hub-in-mindanao-philippines/

———, "Updated Post! OURmindaNOW Summit 2020 in Mindanao, Philippines," webpage, undated b. As of August 7, 2020:
https://www.equalaccess.org/news/
ourmindanow-summit-2020-in-mindanao-philippines/

FAS Intelligence Resource Program, "Alex Boncayao Brigade (ABB)," webpage, May 21, 2004. As of August 7, 2020:
https://fas.org/irp/world/para/abb.htm

Felongco, Gilbert P., "Terror Groups Taking Advantage of Cyberspace for Recruitment," *Gulf News Philippines*, April 27, 2017. As of July 27, 2020:
https://gulfnews.com/news/asia/philippines/
terror-groups-taking-advantage-of-cyberspace-for-recruitment-1.2018173

Ferrer, Raymundo B., and Randolph G. Cabangnag, "Non-International Armed Conflicts in the Philippines," *International Law Studies*, Vol. 88, No. 1, 2012, pp. 263–278.

Fonbuena, Carmela, "Leader of Isis in Philippines Killed, DNA Tests Confirm," *The Guardian*, April 14, 2019. As of August 7, 2020:
https://www.theguardian.com/world/2019/apr/14/
leader-of-isis-in-philippines-killed-dna-tests-confirm

Franco, Joseph, *Marawi: Winning the War After the Battle*, The Hague: International Centre for Counter-Terrorism, November 29, 2017. As of July 18, 2018:
https://icct.nl/publication/marawi-winning-the-war-after-the-battle

———, "Preventing Other 'Marawis' in the Southern Philippines," *Asia and the Pacific Policy Studies*, Vol. 5, No. 2, 2018, pp. 362–369.

Gartenstein-Ross, Daveed, and Colin P. Clarke, "What Do Returning Isis Fighters Do Next? You're About to Find Out," *This Week in Asia*, February 2, 2020. As of August 7, 2020:
https://www.scmp.com/week-asia/opinion/article/3048468/
what-do-asias-returning-isis-fighters-do-next-youre-about-find

Gartenstein-Ross, Daveed, Colin P. Clarke, and Samuel Hodgson, *Foreign Terrorist Fighters from Southeast Asia: What Happens Next?* The Hague: International Center for Counter-Terrorism, February 17, 2020. As of August 7, 2020:
https://icct.nl/publication/
foreign-terrorist-fighters-from-southeast-asia-what-happens-next/

Gutierrez, Jason, "Duterte Says Martial Law in Southern Philippines Will End This Month," *New York Times*, December 10, 2019.

Hart, Michael, "A Year After Marawi, What's Left of ISIS in the Philippines?" *The Diplomat*, October 25, 2018. As of August 7, 2020:
https://thediplomat.com/2018/10/
a-year-after-marawi-whats-left-of-isis-in-the-philippines

———, "With Autonomy in the Philippines, Muslim Rebels Must Learn How to Govern," *World Politics Review*, February 12, 2019. As of August 7, 2020:
https://www.worldpoliticsreview.com/articles/27415/with-autonomy-in-the-southern-philippines-muslim-rebels-must-learn-how-to-govern

Head, Jonathan, "Maute Rebel Group: A Rising Threat to Philippines," *BBC News*, May 31, 2017. As of July 18, 2018:
https://www.bbc.com/news/world-asia-40103602

Huesca, Elieso F., Jr., "On 'Youth, Peace, and Security' in Mindanao, Philippines," *Peace Review*, Vol. 31, 2019, pp. 57–65.

Hutchcroft, Paul, *Mindanao: The Long Journey to Peace and Prosperity*, Mandaluyong, Philippines: Anvil Publishing, 2016.

Hwang, Julie Chernov, "Relatives, Redemptions, and Rice: Motivations for Joining the Maute Group," *CTC Sentinel*, Vol. 12, No. 8, September 2019.

I Am Mindanao, homepage, undated. As of July 18, 2018:
https://iammindanao.wordpress.com

Impl. Project, "2017 Annual Data Review: Marawi and Suburbs, Southern Philippines," briefing, 2017a.

———, "Radicalization Trends and Findings in Mindanao," briefing, 2017b.

Institute for Autonomy and Governance, *Research on Youth Vulnerability to Violent Extremism in the Autonomous Region in Muslim Mindanao*, Cotabato City, Philippines, 2017.

Institute for Economics and Peace, *Global Terrorism Index 2019: Measuring the Index of Terrorism*, Sydney, November 2019. As of August 7, 2020:
http://visionofhumanity.org/app/uploads/2019/11/GTI-2019web.pdf

International Crisis Group, "Tracking Conflict Worldwide," webpage, undated. As of August 7, 2020:
https://www.crisisgroup.org/crisiswatch/
print?page=1&location%5B0%5D=46&t=CrisisWatch+Database+Filter

International Crisis Group, *The Philippines: Renewing Prospects for Peace in Mindanao*, Brussels, Asia Report No. 281, July 6, 2016. As of July 18, 2018:
http://www.refworld.org/pdfid/577e22114.pdf

———, *The Philippines: Militancy and the New Bangsamoro*, Brussels, Asia Report No. 301, July 27, 2019. As of August 7, 2020:
https://d2071andvip0wj.cloudfront.net/301-the-new-bangsamoro.pdf

International Institute for Strategic Studies, *Asia-Pacific Regional Security Assessment 2018*, Washington, D.C., June 2018.

James, Ross W., Ella Romo-Murphy, and Mae-Mosette Oczon-Quirante, "A Realist Evaluation of a Community-Centered Radio Initiative for Health and Development in Mindanao, Philippines," *Asia Pacific Journal of Public Health*, Vol. 31, No. 6, 2019, pp. 559–571.

Jannaral, Julmunir I., "7 Maute Brothers Confirmed Dead," *Manila Times*, December 6, 2017. As of July 18, 2018:
https://www.manilatimes.net/2017/12/06/news/
top-stories/7-maute-brothers-confirmed-dead/366928

Johnston, Patrick B., and Colin P. Clarke, "Is the Philippines the Next Caliphate?" *Foreign Policy*, November 27, 2017. As of August 7, 2020:
https://foreignpolicy.com/2017/11/27/is-the-philippines-the-next-caliphate/

Jones, Clarke R., and Resurrecion S. Morales, "Integration Versus Segregation: A Preliminary Examination of Philippine Correctional Facilities for De-Radicalization," *Studies in Conflict and Terrorism*, Vol. 35, No. 3, 2012, pp. 211–228.

Kruglanski, Arie W., Michele J. Gelfand, Anna Shreveland, Maxim Babush, Malkanthi Hetiarachchi, Michele Ng Bonto, and Rohan Gunaratna, "What a Difference Two Years Make: Patterns of Radicalization in a Philippine Jail," *Dynamics of Asymmetric Conflict*, Vol. 9, Nos. 1–3, 2016, pp. 13–36.

Legaspi, Amita, "AFP Adopts New Security Plan Under Duterte," *GMA News Online*, January 6, 2017. As of July 18, 2018:
http://www.gmanetwork.com/news/news/nation/594904/
afp-adopts-new-security-plan-under-duterte/story

Lopez, Alexander, "Army, IP Leaders Hit NPA Attack on Civilians in Surigao Sur," Philippines News Agency, February 24, 2020. As of August 7, 2020:
https://www.pna.gov.ph/articles/1094706

Lurie, Devin, "ISIS in the Philippines: A Cause for Concern," American Security Project, June 4, 2020. As of August 7, 2020:
https://www.americansecurityproject.org/
isis-in-the-philippines-a-cause-for-concern/

Macapagal, Maan, "PNP-SAF Forms 5 New Battalions, Focuses on Urban Warfare Training," *ABS-CBN News*, May 9, 2018. As of July 18, 2018:
http://news.abs-cbn.com/news/05/08/18/
pnp-saf-forms-5-new-battalions-focuses-on-urban-warfare-training

Mackenzie Institute, "Terrorism Profiles: Abu Sayyaf Group," webpage, last updated November 13, 2015. As of August 11, 2020:
https://mackenzieinstitute.com/terrorism-profile-abu-sayyaf-group-asg/

MacKinnon, Ian, "Philippine Islamists Post Fundraising Clip on YouTube," *The Guardian*, August 20, 2007. As of July 18, 2018:
https://www.theguardian.com/media/2007/aug/20/digitalmedia.internationalnews

Mendez, Christina, and Pia Lee-Brago, "Duterte, Indonesian Envoy Vow Closer Bilateral Cooperation," *Philippine Star*, January 5, 2018. As of July 18, 2018:
https://www.philstar.com/headlines/2018/01/05/1774810/
duterte-indonesian-envoy-vow-closer-bilateral-cooperation

Mogato, Manuel, and Karen Lema, "Philippine Muslims Fear Marawi Fighting May Deepen Communal Discord," Reuters, June 28, 2017. As of July 27, 2020:
https://www.reuters.com/article/us-philippines-militants-muslims/philippine-
muslims-fear-marawi-fighting-may-deepen-communal-discord-idUSKBN19J132

"The New People's Army," *Terrorism*, Vol. 13, No. 2, 1990, pp. 177–181.

O'Brien, McKenzie, "Fluctuations Between Crime and Terror: The Case of Abu Sayyaf's Kidnapping Activities," *Terrorism and Political Violence*, Vol. 24, No. 2, 2012, pp. 320–336.

Office of Presidential Adviser on the Peace Process, "Payapa at Masaganang Pamayanan (PAMANA)," webpage, November 14, 2016. As of July 18, 2018:
https://peace.gov.ph/2016/11/payapa-masaganang-pamayanan-pamana

"Outcome Document: The Role of Parliamentarians in Preventing and Countering Terrorism and Addressing Conditions Conducive to Terrorism in the Asia-Pacific Region," Inter-Parliamentary Union–United Nations Regional Conference, Kuala Lumpur, October 1–3, 2019. As of August 11, 2020:
https://www.un.org/counterterrorism/sites/www.un.org.counterterrorism/files/
outcome_ipu-un_regional_conference_malaysia_oct2019.pdf

Pareño, Roel, "Abu Sayyaf on Recruitment Spree," *Philstar Global*, January 21, 2016. As of July 20, 2018:
https://www.philstar.com/nation/2016/01/21/1544956/
abu-sayyaf-recruitment-spree

Paul, Christopher, Colin P. Clarke, Beth Grill, and Molly Dunigan, *Paths to Victory: Lessons from Modern Insurgencies*, Santa Monica, Calif.: RAND Corporation, RR-291/1-OSD, 2013. As of June 26, 2020:
https://www.rand.org/pubs/research_reports/RR291z1.html

Peace Direct, "The Bishop-Ulama Conference (BUC)," webpage, last updated December 2015. As of July 18, 2018:
https://www.peaceinsight.org/conflicts/philippines/peacebuilding-organisations/
the-bishop-ulama-conference-buc/

Pedroza, Stephen J., "I Am Mindanao Campaign Goes Global," Xavier University, press release, June 30, 2017a. As of August 11, 2020:
https://www.xu.edu.ph/
xavier-news/63-2017-2018/2607-i-am-mindanao-campaign-goes-global

————, "'I Am Mindanao' Campaign Among Final Four in Digital Challenge," Republic of the Philippines Philippine Information Agency, July 3, 2017b. As of July 18, 2018:
https://pia.gov.ph/news/articles/1001960

Philippine Embassy in Washington DC, USA, "#OgopMarawi (Help Marawi)," Facebook post, June 30, 2017. As of August 20, 2020:
https://www.facebook.com/PHinUSA/photos/ogopmarawi-help-marawithe-philippine-army-in-partnership-with-local-non-governme/1932886856725289/

Philippine National Police, *Annual Report 2016*, Quezon City, undated. As of July 18, 2018:
http://www.pnp.gov.ph/images/publications/AR2016.pdf

Philippine Statistics Authority, Region XI—Davao Region, "Factsheet on Islam in Mindanao," webpage, September 28, 2017. As of July 18, 2018:
http://rsso11.psa.gov.ph/article/factsheet-islam-mindanao

"Philippines: Bomb Attack on Davao Market Kills 14," *BBC News*, September 3, 2016. As of August 7, 2020:
https://www.bbc.com/news/world-asia-37262499

"Philippines' Duterte to Lift Martial Law by Year's End," *Al Jazeera*, December 10, 2020. As of August 7, 2020:
https://www.aljazeera.com/news/2019/12/philippines-duterte-lift-law-martial-mindanao-year-191210053427480.html

Regencia, Ted, "Delay in Return 'Boosts ISIL Recruitment' in Philippines' Marawi," *Al Jazeera*, October 22, 2019. As of August 7, 2020:
https://www.aljazeera.com/news/2019/10/delay-return-boosting-isil-recruitment-philippines-marawi-191022063320387.html

Republic of the Philippines, "Republic of the Philippines Bangsamoro Autonomous Region in Muslim Mindanao," webpage, undated. As of August 12, 2020:
https://bangsamoro.gov.ph

————, Republic Act No. 9372, An Act to Secure the State and Protect Our People from Terrorism, 2007.

Republic of the Philippines Department of Foreign Affairs, "Philippines Co-Hosts Workshop on Mainstreaming the Prevention of Violent Extremism in the ARF Region in Brussels," press release, February 27, 2017. As of August 12, 2020:
https://www.dfa.gov.ph/dfa-news/news-from-our-foreign-service-postsupdate/11805-philippines-co-hosts-workshop-on-mainstreaming-the-prevention-of-violent-extremism-in-the-arf-region-in-brussels

Rhoades, Ashley L., Todd C. Helmus, James V. Marrone, Victoria M. Smith, and Elizabeth Bodine-Baron, *Promoting Peace as the Antidote to Violent Extremism: Evaluation of a Philippines-Based Tech Camp Training and Peace Promotion Fellowship*, Santa Monica, Calif.: RAND Corporation, RR-A233-3, 2020. As of August 20, 2020:
http://www.rand.org/pubs/research_reports/RRA233-3.html

Robinson, Linda, Patrick B. Johnston, and Gillian S. Oak, *U.S. Special Operations Forces in the Philippines, 2001–2014*, Santa Monica, Calif.: RAND Corporation, RR-1236-OSD, 2016. As of June 22, 2020:
https://www.rand.org/pubs/research_reports/RR1236.html

Robis, Leah Angela V., "The Sun Rises Anew in Mindanao: Towards Recognizing the Bangsamoro Nation Within the Context of the Philippine Republic," *Ateneo Law Journal*, Vol. 59, No. 4, 2015.

Samuel, Thomas Koruth, *Radicalisation in Southeast Asia: A Selected Case Study of Daesh in Indonesia, Malaysia, and the Philippines*, Kuala Lumpur: Southeast Asia Regional Centre for Counter-Terrorism, 2016.

Sarmiento, Bong S., "ISIS Fading in Mid East, Thriving in the Philippines," *Asia Times*, October 30, 2019. As of August 7, 2020:
https://asiatimes.com/2019/10/isis-fading-in-mid-east-thriving-in-the-philippines

Schuck, Christoph, "How Islamist Is the Abu Sayyaf Group (ASG)? An Ideological Assessment," *Asian Security*, 2020.

Stanford University, Center for International Security and Cooperation, "Mapping Militants—Philippines," data set, undated. As of August 7, 2020:
http://web.stanford.edu/group/mappingmilitants/cgi-bin/maps/view/philippines

———, "Abu Sayyaf Group," webpage, last updated August 2018a. As of July 27, 2020:
http://web.stanford.edu/group/mappingmilitants/cgi-bin/groups/view/152

———, "Bangsamoro Islamic Freedom Fighters," webpage, last updated August 2018b. As of July 27, 2020:
http://web.stanford.edu/group/mappingmilitants/cgi-bin/groups/view/601

———, "Communist Party of the Philippines—New People's Army," webpage, last updated August 2018c. As of July 27, 2020:
http://web.stanford.edu/group/mappingmilitants/cgi-bin/groups/view/149

———, "Moro Islamic Liberation Front," webpage, last updated August 2019a. As of July 27, 2020:
https://cisac.fsi.stanford.edu/mappingmilitants/profiles/
moro-islamic-liberation-front

———, "Moro National Liberation Front," webpage, last updated August 2019b. As of July 27, 2020:
http://web.stanford.edu/group/mappingmilitants/cgi-bin/groups/view/379

Soufan Group, "Islamic State Gains Traction in Southeast Asia," webpage, August 12, 2014. As of July 18, 2018:
http://www.soufangroup.com/
tsg-intelbrief-islamic-state-gains-traction-in-southeast-asia

START—*See* Study of Terrorism and Responses to Terrorism.

START Global Terrorism Database—*See* Study of Terrorism and Responses to Terrorism Global Terrorism Database.

Study of Terrorism and Responses to Terrorism Global Terrorism Database, data set, undated. As of July 18, 2018:
https://www.start.umd.edu/gtd

Sullivan, Colleen, "Alex Boncayo Brigade," *Encyclopedia Britannica*, undated. As of August 7, 2020:
https://www.britannica.com/topic/Alex-Boncayao-Brigade

Temby, Quinton, "Cells, Factions and Suicide Operatives: The Fragmentation of Militant Islamism in the Philippines Post-Marawi," *Contemporary Southeast Asia: A Journal of International and Strategic Affairs*, Vol. 41, No. 1, 2019, pp. 114–137.

Tinnes, Judith, "Although the (Dis-)Believers Dislike It: A Backgrounder on IS Hostage Videos—August–December 2014," *Perspectives on Terrorism*, Vol. 9, No. 1, February 2015.

United Nations Office of the High Commissioner for Human Rights, "UN Special Rapporteur Calls for Changes to the Philippines' Human Security Act," press release, March 12, 2007. As of August 7, 2020:
https://newsarchive.ohchr.org/EN/NewsEvents/Pages/DisplayNews.
aspx?NewsID=1844&LangID=E

United Nations Security Council, Resolution 2178, September 24, 2014. As of July 27, 2020:
https://www.undocs.org/S/RES/2178%20(2014)

Unson, John, "ARMM Turns over Power to Bangsamoro Authority," *Philippine Star*, February 27, 2019. As of August 11, 2020:
https://www.philstar.com/headlines/2019/02/27/1897169/
armm-turns-over-power-bangsamoro-authority

USAID—*See* U.S. Agency for International Development.

U.S. Agency for International Development, "Our Work in Mindanao," webpage, July 6, 2018. As of July 18, 2018:
https://www.usaid.gov/philippines/cross-cutting/mindanao

U.S. Department of Homeland Security, "Countering Violent Extremism Task Force—What Is CVE?" webpage, undated. As of August 7, 2020:
https://www.dhs.gov/cve/what-is-cve

U.S. Department of State, "Programs and Initiatives," webpage, undated. As of August 12, 2020:
https://2009-2017.state.gov/j/ct/programs/index.htm

———, "Building a Global Movement to Address Violent Extremism," fact sheet, September 2015. As of July 18, 2018:
https://2009-2017.state.gov/r/pa/prs/ps/2015/09/247449.htm

———, *Country Reports on Terrorism 2016*, Washington, D.C., 2016. As of August 20, 2020:
https://www.state.gov/reports/country-reports-on-terrorism-2016

———, *Country Reports on Terrorism 2018*, Washington, D.C., 2018. As of August 11, 2020:
https://www.state.gov/reports/country-reports-on-terrorism-2018

U.S. Department of State, Bureau of Counterterrorism, "Foreign Terrorist Organizations," webpage, undated. As of July 27, 2020:
https://www.state.gov/j/ct/rls/other/des/123085.htm

U.S. Department of State, Bureau of Democracy, Human Rights and Labor, *Philippine 2013 International Religious Freedom Report*, Washington, D.C., 2013. As of July 27, 2020:
https://2009-2017.state.gov/documents/organization/222373.pdf

U.S. Indo-Pacific Command, "Pacific Special Operations Forces Sponsor Countering Violent Extremism Workshop in Guam," press release, Camp H. M. Smith, Hawaii, May 31, 2017. As of July 18, 2018:
http://www.pacom.mil/Media/News/News-Article-View/Article/1198414/pacific-special-operations-forces-sponsor-countering-violent-extremism-workshop

U.S. Senate, *U.S. Government Efforts to Counter Violent Extremism*, Washington, D.C.: U.S. Government Printing Office, 2010. As of July 18, 2018:
https://www.gpo.gov/fdsys/pkg/CHRG-111shrg63687/html/CHRG-111shrg63687.htm

Valente, Catherine S., "Duterte to Military: Crush NPA, Other Enemies," *Manila Times*, December 18, 2019. As of August 7, 2020:
https://www.manilatimes.net/2019/12/18/news/top-stories/duterte-to-military-crush-npa-other-enemies/665253/

Vergani, Matteo, "Neojihadism and Muslim–Christian Relations in the Mindanao Resistance Movement: A Study of Facebook Digital Narratives," *Islam and Christian–Muslim Relations*, Vol. 25, No. 3, 2014, pp. 357–372.

Vergani, Matteo, Muhammad Iqbal, Ekin Ilbahar, and Greg Barton, "The Three Ps of Radicalization: Push, Pull, and Personal. A Systematic Scoping Review of the Scientific Evidence About Radicalization into Violent Extremism," *Studies in Conflict and Terrorism*, 2018.

Villamor, Felipe, "Philippines Says It Killed ISIS-Linked Leader in Push to Reclaim City," *New York Times*, October 16, 2017. As of July 18, 2018: https://www.nytimes.com/2017/10/16/world/asia/philippines-marawi-isis-isnilon-hapilon.html

Wakefield, Francis, "Government Troops Still Chasing 150 Abu Sayyaf Terrorists—Lorenzana," *Manila Bulletin*, August 28, 2018. As of August 7, 2020: https://web.archive.org/web/20190109020600/https:/news.mb.com.ph/2018/08/28/government-troops-still-chasing-150-abu-sayyaf-terrorists-lorenzana/

Weiss, Caleb, "Philippines-Based Jihadist Groups Pledge Allegiance to the Islamic State," *FDD's Long War Journal*, February 14, 2016a. As of July 18, 2018: https://www.longwarjournal.org/archives/2016/02/philippines-based-jihadist-groups-pledge-allegiance-to-the-islamic-state.php

——— "Filipino Troops Battle Islamic State–Loyal Forces for Town," Threat Matrix: A Blog of *FDD's Long War Journal*, November 29, 2016b. As of August 7, 2020: https://www.longwarjournal.org/archives/2016/11/filipino-troops-battle-islamic-state-loyal-forces-for-town.php

Windrem, Robert, "ISIS Recruits Fighters for the Philippines Instead of Syria," *NBC News*, September 12, 2017. As of July 27, 2020: https://www.nbcnews.com/storyline/isis-uncovered/isis-recruits-fighters-philippines-instead-syria-n796741

World Bank, "Philippines: Autonomous Region in Muslim Mindanao (ARMM Social Fund Project)," webpage, April 10, 2013. As of July 18, 2018: http://www.worldbank.org/en/results/2013/04/10/philippines-autonomous-region-in-muslim-mindanao-social-fund-project

Yusa, Zam, "Philippines: 100 Foreign Fighters Joined ISIS in Mindanao Since the Marawi Battle," *Defense Post*, November 5, 2018. As of August 7, 2020: https://www.thedefensepost.com/2018/11/05/100-foreign-fighters-join-isis-mindanao-philippines-marawi